LEAN OUT

LEAN
OUT

The Struggle for Gender Equality
in Tech and Start-Up Culture

EDITED BY

ELISSA
SHEVINSKY

OR Books
New York · London

Published by OR Books, New York and London
Visit our website at www.orbooks.com

All rights information: rights@orbooks.com

First printing 2015

Cataloging-in-Publication data is available from the Library of Congress. A catalog record for this book is available from the British Library.

ISBN 978-1-939293-86-2 paperback
ISBN 978-1-939293-87-9 e-book

Text design by Bathcat Ltd. Typeset by AarkMany Media, Chennai, India. Printed by BookMobile in the United States and CPI Books Ltd. in the United Kingdom. The U.S. printed edition of this book comes on Forest Stewardship Council-certified, 30% recycled paper. The printer, BookMobile, is 100% wind-powered.

"I love to see a young girl go out and grab the world by the lapels. Life's a bitch. You've got to go out and kick ass."
—Maya Angelou

CONTENTS

INTRODUCTION
Elissa Shevinsky

Silicon Valley has risen to mainstream importance—and so has its gender problem. White male subcultures have come to dominate the landscape of startups and blue chip tech companies. The success of men like Apple co-founder Steve Jobs and Facebook CEO Mark Zuckerberg created the perception that ideal founders of companies look just like they did—young, white, male, and socially awkward.

This myth of the nerdy male founder has been perpetuated by men who found this story favorable. Paul Graham, one of Silicon Valley's most influential investors, said in an interview in 2014:

> God knows what you would do to get 13-year-old girls interested in computers . . . We can't make these women look at the world through hacker eyes and start Facebook because they haven't been hacking for the past 10 years.

John Doerr, a partner at the Venture Capital firm Kleiner Perkins, sang the praises of the legendary young white male nerd at the National Venture Capital Association's annual meeting in 2008:

> In the early days when you went back in the Amazon shipping area, the books were lined up so you could see what people were buying. Invariably there was a book about programming language like Java, and in the same sales order there was a book like *The Joy of Sex*. These [customers] were probably very clearly male, nerds who had no social or sex lives trying to get help by using an online service.

> That correlates more with any other success factor that I've seen in the world's greatest entrepreneurs. If you look at Bezos, or [Netscape Communications Corp. founder] Marc Andreessen, [Yahoo Inc. co-founder] David Filo, the founders of Google, they all seem to be white, male, nerds who've dropped out of Harvard or Stanford and they absolutely have no social life. So when I see that pattern coming in— which was true of Google—it was very easy to decide to invest.

Things may be getting better for women and minorities in tech but the damage that has been done is substantial. The "pattern recognition" in favor of young white male nerds is deeply ingrained.

The worst part about this myth is that it is blatantly untrue. Jobs and Zuckerberg did not build their companies by themselves. Women played irreplaceable roles at Apple and at Facebook. Photographs and documentary records of the early days at those companies show women as critical parts of the founding teams. Their stories have been carefully erased by men like Zuckerberg and Jobs, who are both widely acknowledged to be masterful storytellers.

Even the *New York Times*, in a June 2012 article on gender issues in Silicon Valley[1] proclaimed that the Internet was built by men. Pulitzer Prize–winning journalist David Streitfeld wrote "MEN invented the Internet. And not just any men. Men with pocket protectors. Men who idolized Mr. Spock and cried when Steve Jobs died. Nerds. Geeks. Give them their due."

Despite his impressive credentials, Streitfeld was not correct. Men did not build the Internet, at least not without women. Judith Estrin was one of the key designers of TCP/IP, which is one of the main building blocks ("protocols," to be precise) for communicating information over the Internet. Radia Perlman invented STP, critical for modern networking. Perlman's contribution was significant enough that she has been called the "Mother of the Internet." Perlman resisted this title, saying "The Internet was not invented by any

---

[1] http://www.nytimes.com/2012/06/03/technology/lawsuit-against-kleiner-perkins-is-shaking-silicon-valley.html

individual." She also noted "There are lots of people who like to take credit for it, and it drives them crazy when anyone other than them seems to want credit, so it seems best to just stay out of their way."[2]

The list goes on. Glenda Schroeder made the first command-line, and also authored one of the earliest research papers proposing a method for creating electronic mail (e-mail) back in the nineteen sixties. Sandra Lerner co-founded Cisco Systems, and co-designed the first Cisco router. Nicola Pellow wrote the first cross-platform web browser, which made the web accessible to consumers, beyond its original limited applications in military and academia.

And of course, let's not forget Ada Lovelace. Ada is widely acknowledged to be the founder of "scientific computing"—or programming, as we call it today. Yes, the very first programmer was a woman.

Women were essential to the development of programming, computing, and the Internet itself. Unfortunately, they weren't the loudest about it and so they have been all but erased from our narrative of who gets to lay claim to technology and its culture.

This kind of erasure persists today. Whitney Wolfe sued her cofounders at Tinder for sexual discrimination/harassment—and for their efforts to erase her from the company history. According to the lawsuit, Tinder CMO

---

[2] http://www.theatlantic.com/technology/archive/2014/03/radia-perlman-dont-call-me-the-mother-of-the-internet/284146/

Justin Matteen said "Facebook and Snapchat doesn't have girl founders, it just makes it look like Tinder was some accident." Wolfe and Tinder settled out of court, but it is now widely acknowledged that she was a founder, prior to her departure from the company.

The movies and history books and hiring practices at big tech companies may reinforce the idea that young white male nerds have a natural affinity with computers and with code. But the truth is that women—and women who defied their assigned gender roles at great cost—have just as rightful a place among the luminaries of Silicon Valley.

If this book matters, it's because we are part of a movement to tell the untold stories.

*

Lean Out is a manifesto, written by some of the most thoughtful and powerful voices in the emerging feminist/intersectional movement. The essays in this text represent the views of each author alone, though of course with the support and blessing of both me and OR Books.

Lauren Bacon was the first writer who I asked to join this project. Her writing is thoughtful and full of insight, and she shares my vision for a passionate but moderate feminism. I'm grateful to her for saying "yes" at a moment when this book was just a hope. It is a tremendous privilege to publish her and to be counted among her collaborators.

Katy Levinson was one of the first people to welcome me to Silicon Valley, through her work at The Hacker Dojo. The Hacker Dojo, in its heyday, was a warm and welcoming coworking and community space in Mountain View. Katy was an important figure in the community, always dedicated to making good things happen. Her piece on feminists as whistleblowers is required reading for understanding what is at stake for women who speak out.

It was Katy Levinson who first introduced me to FAKEGRIMLOCK. She described FAKEGRIMLOCK as an Internet famous robot dinosaur, which is an entirely accurate description. There is so much to love about GRIMLOCK's message. Perhaps the best thing is how GRIMLOCK could be anyone. GRIMLOCK is a dinosaur! Could be male, female, or neither.

This book explores the question of whether technology deserves women and minorities. GRIMLOCK's essays remind me that technology is too important for us to ignore and that innovation belongs to all of us. To quote the robot dinosaur, "YOU BELONG IN TECH."

The challenge then is how to navigate the landscape—how to create our own cultures, how to find companies where we fit in, so we can lead and not follow. So we can belong.

Dom DeGuzman is a software engineer at Twilio, and a frequent speaker on the experience of being LGBTQ in tech. Besides being incredibly talented, Dom is a kind of "everywoman success story," much needed at a moment when we are so desperate for positive role models. Dom experienced the best and the worst of life as a female programmer before ultimately finding a warm and productive home at Twilio. She is fearless about sharing those experiences with the rest of us. I'm learning a lot from her.

I was introduced to Squinky by Nicky Case, a mutual friend. Squinky is a beloved indie game developer. The standard post on a VC or tech blog is all about figuring out how to make something that people want. But for many of us, creation is easy. It's navigating our way through cultural fit, through corporate life, that is hard. Squinky's writing speaks to everyone who sees the world as an artist or activist, and to everyone who knows what it's like to just not fit in.

Brook Shelley writes about being transgender. Having been perceived by people as both male and female, Brook speaks with unique authority about gender bias. Brook's story is a must-read for insights into how gender impacts one's experience as a technologist.

Sunny Allen is a cofounder at HUM, as well as the face of the brand. HUM is the first artificially-intelligent vibrator. Allen came to my attention after she was named a woman worth her tech salt by Debrief (British version of Jezebel online), in their feminist response to *Forbes'* overwhelmingly male "30 under 30" list of impressive people in consumer tech.

Sunny writes with much-needed honesty about the darker aspects of life as a startup founder.

As we started to put together this anthology, a string of stories broke about women in tech being sexually harassed. I wish that their stories were unique. Rather it's their willingness to come forward—and their grace and eloquence in telling their stories—that is distinctive.

Gesche Haas was told by a prominent VC that he simply would not leave Berlin without having sex with her. Haas tells her story—and the aftermath of speaking out—in depth here for the first time. Gesche is leading a movement of women founders, called "Dreams & Doers."

Emily Swallow joined the VC firm General Catalyst as a summer intern. She was idealistic and optimistic, and excited about identifying potential female founders for investment opportunities. Her ideas were shut down, and Swallow was "constantly reminded of her place as a woman in a man's world." With very few women in the industry, and even fewer willing to speak out about it, Swallow's story is one of the only accounts of sexism within VC firms. Swallow is well-known for her business writing, and her story has already become one of the most iconic accounts of women in Venture Capital.

anna anthropy is a 30-year-old teen witch. She is a play designer, the author of *Rise of the Videogame Zinesters* and *ZZT*, and a game historian, maintaining an archive of game documents and history at annarchive .com. anthropy is beloved by the indie gaming community for exploring dark topics like the relationship between gaming and sadism. She lives in Oakland, California with two gay cats.

I met Krys Freeman through Lesbians Who Tech. Krys has a fire and a civic activism that I find inspiring. I've learned a lot from Krys, because s/he has been unafraid to be straightforward with me. I'm grateful for that.

Erica Joy's piece, "The Other Side of Diversity," came to my attention after it was initially posted on Medium. I thought that it was important and incredibly useful to show what it's like to be at a company like Google as a person of color. This piece is a must-read. Very appreciative that Erica supported including this piece in *Lean Out*.

Leanne Pittsford, founder of Lesbians Who Tech, is building much-needed community for LGBTQ technologists and allies. Men have had their boys club for years. And now LGBTQ women have a community, a home, in Silicon Valley. Leanne is expanding the Lesbians Who Tech summits to include events all over the world. Personally, I believe that it's not enough to critique the existing power structures. We also need to build new communities, new organizations and new infrastructures ourselves. Leanne Pittsford and Lesbians Who Tech are a perfect example.

Jenni Lee is a social entrepreneur, a TedX speaker, the subject of a documentary about adopted Chinese girls, and an advocate for women. Her realism about the changes that we need to see haven't dampened her warmth and enthusiasm for building awesome technology together.

Ash Huang describes herself as "Part wolf, angry American. Independent designer, illustrator, writer." She's done product, design, and branding work for some of the most influential companies in Silicon Valley—Twitter, Pinterest, Dropbox. I admire Ash's ability to navigate these companies gracefully, choosing which clients she will take on and working as she pleases. I look up to Ash as a role model for leaning out—doing things on her own terms—while still being part of the Silicon Valley ecosystem.

Ash and I agreed that we would be friends as introverts do—gently acknowledge mutual respect via video conferences and Twitter faves.

Leigh Alexander is the leading voice in games journalism and games reviewing today, period. She is the Pauline Kael of games, demanding more from a medium she loves and frequently getting it.

Katherine Cross is a beloved feminist writer, a trans Latina, and co-editor of The Border House. She is one of the most articulate and passionate voices on gaming culture and feminist theory. She is one of my only friends and colleagues who regularly receives fan art, inspired by her activism. Cross is working on her PhD at the CUNY Graduate Center.

Melanie Moore is the entrepreneur who originally inspired me to "lean out." I remember her exact words, as she told me her personal philosophy for being happy and successful in tech: "Go around the patriarchy." Hand gestures may have been involved, or it could be my imagination overly romanticizing that moment.

So many of us are fighting, martyring our way through, responding to a male-dominated ecosystem by hitting our heads against one roadblock after another—like so many estrogen-fueled battering rams. Fully appreciating the impact made by the women doing this work, it's not the path that I want for myself. It was Melanie who first taught me that there is another way to be a woman entrepreneur: simply go around the obstacles.

Don't ask for permission. Just go straight for the prize, which is more accessible than you'd think—building a real business, with paying customers.

YOU BELONG IN TECH
FAKEGRIMLOCK, Robot Startup Dinosaur

PEOPLE SAY TECH MOST IMPORTANT THING IN WORLD.
NOT TRUE.
TECH ONLY IMPORTANT THING IN WORLD.
THAT WHY YOU BELONG IN TECH.

YOUR WORLD? ALREADY DEAD. KILLED BY THE
FUTURE. EVERYTHING YOU KNOW, EVERYTHING YOU
HAVE, SOMEONE ELSE ALREADY MADE OBSOLETE.

WITH TECH.

YOUR LIFE, YOUR JOB, YOUR RIGHTS, EVERY DAY
CHANGED BY TECH. EVERY DAY FUTURE ARRIVE
FASTER AND FASTER. EVERY DAY IT BUILT BY FEWER
AND FEWER. UNTIL ONE DAY ONE PERSON CHANGE
ENTIRE WORLD WITH LINE OF CODE.

THAT DAY WAS 10 YEARS AGO.
THAT WHY YOU BELONG IN TECH.

ANGER, COMPLAINTS, DENIAL, DO NOTHING. NO ONE
CAN CHANGE FUTURE AFTER IT GET HERE. BY TIME
YOU ANGRY ABOUT TODAY SOMEONE ELSE ALREADY
BUILT A DIFFERENT TOMORROW. TECH NOT WAIT
FOR YOU. OR FOR ANYONE. TECH ASK NO ONE'S
PERMISSION TO CHANGE THE WORLD.

YOU NEED NO ONE'S PERMISSION EITHER.

IF YOU LET SOMEONE ELSE BUILD TOMORROW,
TOMORROW WILL BELONG TO SOMEONE ELSE. THEY
WILL BUILD A BETTER TOMORROW FOR EVERYONE LIKE
THEM.

YOU CAN HOPE THAT INCLUDE YOU. OR YOU CAN BE THE
ONE THAT BUILD A BETTER TOMORROW WITH YOU IN IT.

THAT WHY YOU BELONG IN TECH.

TECH NEEDS YOU. TECH NEEDS SKILLS. YOU CAN
LEARN THE SKILLS. TECH NEEDS THE BEST. YOU CAN
BE THE BEST. NO ONE STOPPING YOU. FOR TOMORROW
TO BE FOR EVERYONE, EVERYONE NEEDS TO BE THE
ONE THAT BUILD IT.

YOU CAN BE THE ONE THAT CHANGE THE WORLD WITH
A LINE OF CODE. YOU MUST.

HAPPEN TO THE FUTURE.
BEFORE IT HAPPEN TO YOU.

WHAT WE DON'T SAY

Sunny Allen

There is a thing that we all do as startup entrepreneurs—and that's lie, politely. We go to cocktail parties and on dates and post on social media, and make small talk. When asked about our companies, we say we are crushing it. We are crushing it, all the time. But under the surface even successful companies are a mess. And under the surface, so are many founders.

Silicon Valley is just starting to talk about failures, disappointments, darkness—both personal and professional. Prominent Venture Capitalist Brad Feld has written extensively about startup depression and even founder suicide. Robert Scoble came out recently about his early sexual abuse and subsequent addictions.

And here, Sunny Allen—celebrated "30 under 30" entrepreneur, cofounder of the highly-praised artificial intelligence/sex toy company HUM—shares her story.

Listen. There's something more I want to tell you about being an entrepreneur. There's something more I want to tell you about Silicon Valley.

It breaks us. And we become entrepreneurs because we are already broken.

Many of us build companies because we've fucked up our relationships and have nothing else to live for. Some of us are suicidal and the dream of building a better future or getting out of the rat race is the only thing that keeps us going. Most of us are unhappy and when questioned, some of us do not even believe that happiness exists. We are united by two things. A "fuck it" attitude, and the ability to work like dogs.

*

This twenty-one-year-old in khaki shorts and boat shoes was enthusiastically trying to network with me at one of our legendary Sunnyvale hacker house barbecues and I was stoned out of my mind. A few hours earlier I had eaten a marijuana brownie, aka an "edible," bought off an app that delivers weed to your doorstep. In San Francisco, we have apps for getting high.

The kid is moving deliberately through the party asking over and over:

"What's your name? What do you do for a living?"

I somehow manage to tell him I'm cofounder of a robotics startup and his eyes light up. A STARTUP

FOUNDER? HE'S FOUND THE HEART OF SILICON VALLEY! He moves in for the networking.

He tells me his life story. His sophomore class schedule. How much value he got out of English 101. His high school G.P.A. and his SAT score and all of his high school extracurricular activities. I know his hometown and his science fair prowess and his end-of-semester thesis topic. He finally pauses to take a breath, smiling at me triumphantly. Networking achieved.

There's silence for a moment. I lean in, a stupid grin is widening across my face. Words fall out of my mouth. I say, "I feel like you just gave me the elevator pitch for your LIFE, man."

He looks stunned. I feel stunned. But the high does not care. The edible inside me just says, "I gotta go get some ribs off the grill."

I know I was stoned when I was such a dick to that poor kid. I regret doing it—who ever thought I'D be the Silicon Valley insider being an asshole to some college kid in boat shoes?—but stoned or no, there's something here that makes my blood run cold. These outsiders. They come to Silicon Valley and assume that just because I'm a cofounder, I'm rich and successful and my life is glorious.

*

The first day I moved into the battered women's shelter, I had to mop human shit off the floor of the bedroom before I could walk to my bunk.

She was a bloated, pasty woman with all her hair chopped off, standing in the middle of a group of sad quiet women. She was mumbling incoherently, swaying back and forth in a sweatshirt and sweatpants. She was shitting as she stood there. It was falling down her sweatpants and into her shoes, then squishing, slowly, out onto the floor.

She stumbled back to her bunk, leaving brown footprints behind her. We plugged in a fan and the blades began to whir. I picked up a mop.

I could have flown home to Kentucky. I could have slept on my grandmother's couch. But I was trying to build a company.

I was running a DARPA-funded bioreactor project out of Hacker Dojo down in Mountain View. It took me three hours one way to get from the shelter in San Francisco down to Hacker Dojo by public transit.

At the Dojo we'd write code, solder connections, talk about control systems, and gesticulate wildly at the white board while arguing about algae and resource recycling and hydrogen fuel cells and the importance of bioreactors for long-term space travel. On the train home I'd look out the window blankly. In the shelter at night I'd eat Ramen noodles, secretly text my abusive fiancé, finger my beautiful engagement ring, and cry.

*

The bioreactor is this beautiful dream about the world. Microscopic, single-celled algae float around in a glowing glass tank. Sensors flash, motors whir, gases bubble, data flows through the wires. You give the algae all your waste products, the CO_2 you exhale, your piss, your shit, and these little, wet, green circles churn through all of it and give you back the building blocks for human life: oxygen, and a food source, and cleansed water.

I used to watch the algae under the microscope and just marvel. From the outside all you see is this slimy green goo oozing on the top of the lake or clinging to the edge of your fish tank, but slip a few droplets under the microscope and there's this breathtakingly beautiful world hidden in there, this beautiful powerhouse of a world that the rest of the entire ecosystem depends on.

Silicon Valley tends the opposite way. We parade the boundless optimism. We make sure you know how much you all depend on us. We hide everything else.

I had to shut down my bioreactor project because it didn't matter how much NASA and CASIS were interested in funding me to get it up to the space station; I couldn't afford food *now*.

I joined a robotic dildo company instead. At least I could eat. Fuck it.

*

What has Silicon Valley done to me?

Why did I decide that being an entrepreneur was such a good idea?

What are my values?

*

Recently I joined OKCupid. I agreed to meet a guy at a bar in the Mission. He sat down and introduced himself and said he couldn't tell me what his work was because it was special and a secret but he was here tonight with his "work colleagues." I got more and more annoyed as he repeatedly used the phrase "work colleagues" and I finally snapped, "HOW long did you say you've lived in San Francisco?"

"Two days," he said.

"Two DAYS?!?" I repeated. "I can't date you."

He stared at me. "I just took two tequila shots," he explained, "and they were so huge, I don't understand why the bartender—did you just say you can't date me?"

"LOOK," I told him. "The first year I lived in San Francisco I floated on the surface, the second year I got chewed up, and the third year I became a San Franciscan."

Flashback. The hacker house, the weekend before. A woman, still in the beginning of her transition from the male gender, is grinning at the hacker house party. Transgender people move to San Francisco not only for the supposedly (yes, more) positive culture around transitioning, but also for the laws mandating that health insurance cover the hormones necessary for gender dysmorphism disorder.

"I arrived yesterday!" she had told me, grinning, innocent, hopeful, cheerful.

"This city will destroy you. Chew you up and spit you back out," I had told her. I took a sip of bourbon, neat. Her face fell, but I had already turned away.

"I can't date YOU," I said to my date that night in the bar, the tone of my voice rising a little frantically. "You don't know anything about it here. You don't know what it takes. You don't understand the culture. You don't know how to survive, you don't know how hard it is here, or the right things to say, or how you're supposed to talk about stealth startups and you DON'T EVEN KNOW THAT NOBODY SAYS THE PHRASE WORK COL-LEAGUES."

He stared at me some more and blinked a couple times, slowly. Then he leaned in. His nose was getting larger and larger in my face and his palms were coming in toward my cheeks. His lips parted slightly.

"WHAT THE FUCK ARE YOU TRYING TO KISS ME?" I screamed, and stood up. I left the bar.

The next morning I bought a train ticket for Los Angeles. It was time to get out of town.

*

I stared out the window on Amtrak. Gorgeous beaches. Decaying houses. Graffiti on fences, rock formations. Massive bridges. Everything flashed by my windows for twelve hours. A man sat quietly in the cafe car with staff paper spread out across an entire table. He was compos-ing a symphony.

How did I get here? Is Silicon Valley worth as much as I've given it? Am I missing out on the rest of life? Am I wasting my life in this techno-utopian miasma?

I am not entirely sane, I am sometimes self-destructive and often reckless.

I set myself to building companies because it was the most massive thing I could envision doing, because I get bored and restless when I accomplish things easily, and because nothing else in my life even seemed accomplishable.

As I watched life roll past me from the train window, I wondered:

When did I start being such a bitch to people?

But maybe I was missing the point. It's not that I've spontaneously become such a bitch. It's that I've taken on the culture of Silicon Valley, and Silicon Valley is a bitch.

It breaks all of us down. It breaks us.

*

My then-fiancé had been slipping into an Adderall-induced psychosis slowly over the course of the last year. We had moved to San Francisco together so he could work for a typical app-based startup. He was a code monkey. He and his fellow coders competed:

who could write the most lines of code
who could stay up the most days in a row
who could sleep the least number of hours between
    coding sessions

And he who could take the most Adderall was king of the code. My fiancé liked to win.

I was at Hacker Dojo once the next summer. I walked back from lunch to see an ambulance and four police cars out front. The paramedics were wheeling out a young man on a stretcher. I recognized him. He'd been at the Dojo all week, alternating between three states: coding at his laptop, bragging at the top of his lungs about how much code he'd written, and passing out on the couch like he was dead but only for twenty minutes. Soon he'd be shouting into his phone again while typing furiously. As far as I could tell he hadn't left the Dojo in days. The Dojo's open twenty-four hours. Some people live in their cars in the parking lot while they build their apps at the Dojo's long conference tables, around the ping pong table and the empty hardware hacking room. When they pulled him out on the stretcher, he was twitching.

This is Silicon Valley.

We do uppers and write code until they have to pull us out of the Dojo on a stretcher, and we glorify it.

*

I'm an entrepreneur. I've fit the San Francisco definition of homelessness for two years. I've wandered from shelter to couch to hacker house to hacker house.

I'm an entrepreneur. I have a laptop and a patent lawyer who works for equity. What else could I need?

*

On the last day I felt like I had a home, two years ago, I was recovering from surgery on the couch in the living room on the bottom floor of our loft. I couldn't keep down the pain pills they'd given me; I kept throwing them up. I was spiraling downward into this animal world of vomit and increasing pain. I was on the phone to my mother who told me to go to the ER so they could put me on a morphine drip, but my fiancé was refusing to take me.

I didn't understand then that he couldn't see reality clearly any more. He just kept taking his Adderall in the morning and insisting that he could take care of me on his own, while my mother cried on the phone and I begged him to take me to the hospital. Finally I just called an ambulance. As the morphine drip spread into my body I slipped into a state of peace as the doctor's calming voice said, floating above me, "You were right to come here. We can help you. Sleep."

My fiancé tracked me down at the hospital and drove me home again. I slept, again on the couch, but this time with a bottle of anti-nausea pills clutched to my chest. My fiancé leaned over the stair railing from the second story of our beautiful loft, he leaned his chest way out over the railing until his face was right over me where I was laying on the couch, and then he spit on me. "To punish me," he said. "For going to the hospital," he said.

*

Think about Silicon Valley as a race up a mountain. There's a suite of traditional prizes, like owning a Tesla and the social currency of tech fame that gets you invited to the best parties. There is the question of which Burning Man camp you camp with, and which corporate cafeterias you eat at. How many fancy bottles of bourbon do you have on a cart next to your desk? Then of course there is the granddaddy of tech wins—the entrepreneur's IPO. This leads to "fuck you money."

There's a traditional way to run the race, too. A boy's club, although women can join if they do it just right. This involves going to Stanford (MIT is also acceptable) and networking events and joining Angel List and having great recommendations on your LinkedIn profile. At cocktail parties you talk about lean pivots and the importance of a Good Team. You are young and white and gorgeous. Or as gorgeous as nerds ever get to be. You wore glasses until you got lasik. There is a thing called pattern recognition, there is a thing that Venture Capitalists and Hiring Managers look for. And I am not that thing.

I was not in the race. I was at the bottom of a very large hole. All I knew was that I needed to climb out somehow. One day I realized that I'd gotten so good at climbing out of the hole that I'd accidentally climbed half way up the back side of the mountain.

Co-founder! Entrepreneur! I did it! I'm one a y'all bitches.

I sign NDAs, I own stock, I build robots, journalists call me for quotes, they talk about me on TV, I'm at the hottest table at the hottest parties, I'm snorting coke and ketamine, I go home with the DJ, I have followers on Facebook, people email asking to buy me coffee, they wanna hear my advice, I'm a fucking lingerie model, I call my mother and tell her I only date models, my grandmother calls me in tears after reading my Facebook to ask what monster I've become. I just laugh at her. I so, just laugh at her.

Who can expect an eighty-six-year-old woman in a retirement home in Kentucky to understand who I've become in Silicon Valley?

"If this is what happens to young women there, then young women should be banned from the State of California!" she declares. Then sobs. I hang up.

*

Here's an excerpt from the email I sent my grandmother to announce my engagement three years ago:

> *"Then Michael hailed a taxi and took us to the Palace of Fine Arts. It was built for the 1915 World's Fair in San Francisco, and it was designed to look like the ruins from a Roman temple. During the day, while the museum and theatre are open inside, it's a very popular, crowded tourist destination. At night however, it was completely empty. The "ruins" were beautifully, sparsely lit, and the only sounds were*

our own footfalls and the quiet noises of a few birds still awake on the waters of the lagoon.

He proposed to me outside the dome, on a path by the water. He went down on one knee, but he was so flustered that he forgot to ask the question. So I just said yes!

Afterwards, he ordered another car which took us to the Hyatt downtown. He had made reservations for drinks and dessert at a restaurant on the top floor of the hotel. We could see the entire city from the windows. We ordered caramel ice cream and creme brûlée, and real French champagne. The champagne smelled like roses."

*

Did my fiancé already have violent tendencies. Yes. Did my fiancé already have a history of psychosis. Yes. Was our engagement already doomed, and us a terrible match, and me far too restless to ever be happy in a traditional marriage? Yes, yes, and yes.

But did Silicon Valley break us and abuse us and kill our souls? Yes.

*

I went on a date with one of my mentors last summer. In Silicon Valley you start a crush by copying his business model. I was crazy about him because he wrote about his life and work with so much honest vulnerability; he was so willing to plunge into the dark recesses of his life and talk about how it'd all inspired him to explore the beauty in the world. He wrote about how he'd been brutally dumped, and homeless, and he realized how empty and devoid of skills and value his old career had been, and so then he set out to find a better way to live in the world. But on the date he just snorted.

"I checked off all the boxes," he said. "My company is both open-source and profitable. I just closed a round of funding. I wrote a book. I did a TED talk. I've been to the White House. And none of it has satisfied me. I just wish I could quit all of it and start a family."

The rest of the date, he spent fifty percent talking about how much he wanted a family, and the other fifty percent telling me how much he needed to live alone.

I've thought about his contradictions many times—how dissatisfied he was in real life as compared to the boundless wonder and optimism in his public writings.

How, upon achieving success, he was convinced that the real success was somewhere else. If only he could just track down that next thing.

*

We're Silicon Valley entrepreneurs. We're making it. What are we all searching for? What makes us so restless?

Why are we all so unhappy?
Is this all there is?
Is it worth it?

*

Kate Heddleston wrote a paragraph critiquing *Lean In* that haunts me:

Women in tech are the canary in the coal mine. Normally when the canary in the coal mine starts dying you know the environment is toxic and you should get the hell out. Instead, the tech industry is looking at the canary, wondering why it can't breathe, saying "Lean in, canary. Lean in!" When one canary dies they get a new one because getting more canaries is how you fix the lack of canaries, right? Except the problem is that there isn't enough oxygen in the coal mine, not that there are too few canaries.

My name is Sunny Allen. I'm a woman and a Silicon Valley entrepreneur. I'm also a Kentucky McCoy and my great-great-grandfathers all died of black lung in the coal mines that powered the Industrial Revolution.

I don't know much. I often feel lost. But I know this: I'm a Silicon Valley entrepreneur. I'm a coal miner. I am powering the revolution.

THE OTHER WOMEN
Leigh Alexander

*As feminists, we can become so embattled that we end up
fighting amongst ourselves. We see enemies where there
are friends, or potential friends. This essay by Leigh
Alexander rings all too true.*

Like lots of people who eventually become activists, I
wasn't much interested in feminism until problems came
to my own door. I was a bootstrapper, you see, I was one
of the few women actually doing writing about video
games, and I didn't think much about why there were so
few of us. I was partially aware of some of the challenges
posed by my rarity, but, you know, I wanted to "focus on
my work." I wanted to avoid "making it about" my gender.

I felt tough. And secretly, I probably liked my rarity. There's this dance two women in a male-dominated

field will do when men introduce them. At first you feel resentful: *does he want me to meet her just because we're both women?* And then, it's like, *who's she*, and has she paid the same high cost as I paid, or is she just in here because she's pretty?

You shake hands with her, hard, and you smile a lot because you're supposed to support other women. But privately you watch her out of the corner of your eye, inexplicably a little bit threatened—even after you've learned and you know better. You can't undo your mistrust so easily. Your colleague becomes an emblem of a flawed system. Is she a *good feminist*, or one of those scabs? Is she better than you, do the men like her better than you?

I didn't like that dance, and I didn't like the bad feelings about myself that came with it. So I just didn't think about women in games, for a while. I had lots of cool and funny and great and supportive men friends, so I cleaved closely to them, preferred them, even emulated them, like one of those scabs. And then, I got successful. I became a woman who sticks her head over the line, and I learned about the consequences for that. And I saw how many of my cool, supportive, funny dude friends shrunk away helplessly from the ways women are targeted by audiences in our fields.

It becomes like finding a fuse buried in the dust. A tiny glimpse of red cord you notice almost by accident, and that you pull until you start to unspool this entire lethal infrastructure that has you in its crosshairs. Things are not fair for you. Things have never been fair for you.

The words that will be used on you will be different, worse. The way your audience treats you will suddenly infuriate you in a million tiny ways that seem unreasonable to men, because, *like, dude, they're not saying you're lying or something*, it's just, they've never *seen* it, and so maybe you should be less sensitive and more community-minded.

Community-minded. The only thing that's as bad as finding out that someone has put weights in your gear, or has been handicapping your score, is finding that others have it even worse. You learn about marginalized women, people with bigger fears and problems than not being invited to the right open bar or having too many mansplaining Twitter followers. You dine on your own guilt at ever having excluded *anybody*, but most especially other women, from your dude friends' guest lists. So you decide to start trying to help fix things.

You engage in occasional hashtag activism. You start to talk about the big F-word. You're relieved that there is a name for the hostile infrastructure you always sensed on your periphery, but didn't want to believe was real. You want to share, without stopping to think, this thudding adrenaline flood with the other women, who you presume are gonna be *so stoked*. You expect that they will forgive you straight away for how you were. They often do, but sometimes they don't. You volunteer to help out at a conference's advocacy track. You invite all the marginalized women you can think of and you glow with warmth. You can finally make them happy.

At the conference they are all still mad.

You don't get it. You did such a good job listening. Aren't they supposed to say thank you? All of your fellow advocates are frustrated. They just must not understand what you are trying to do, here. You consider writing an email: *"Dear so and so, I just want to make sure you understand—"* A softly-blinking man in a clean shirt with a fatherly mien sighs because he has known this woman or that woman for many years and he says that while she means well, she is *just difficult*. You are trying to *save* people and they don't even *appreciate* it. After a while you start to understand that others' anger at the infra-structure is not something you can people-please away. This is not a game where you're a hero, jumping atop the heads of all the unjust, saving the princesses waiting for their chance to be heard.

After a while, you get angry that anyone has that very idea. They tell your friends to calm down and to get along and before long, you are angry, too. Things start to cohere for you when you get angry. Anger is the main thing you have in common with the other women, despite all your manifold privileges, experiences or lack thereof, and everyone—all these guys, mostly—want you to calm down and let go of it.

You don't let go. You yank that wire until the whole virulent, softly-blinking machine looms over your dust-smudged face, within reach of your split knuckles.

Recently I was done an injustice by a company. In the ensuing discussions about rectifying injustices, several colleagues reached out to me worriedly. They just wanted to *make sure I understood* what they were trying to *achieve*, with all their grand plans that did not include me. It was the first time in my life I really knew the taste of bile, the distinct rage others among my colleagues, women and nonbinary and otherwise marginalized colleagues alike, must have been experiencing for years, corralled into advocacy tracks by people who treated them as if they knew the solutions best of all. Doing work to help us, without asking us.

We are up against so much, even from people who really want to help, even from other women who are just a little bit more privileged or successful than we are. But at every games event I go to, when I drink with the women who are my friends, the truth always comes out: The people we are most afraid of in our professional spaces are almost always, always other women—more so the closer to our own demographic they are. That criticism, the lack of advocacy, fractured or insincere solidarity always hurts the most when it comes from people who are the most like ourselves. And further, we recruit one another into the service of policing each other's feminism rather than in constructively helping one another through the unfair system.

Are we still doing that too-hard handshake? Are we still acting out the microaggressions, the condescension, that we learned from the people in power? How can we ever hope that game and technology conferences will be safe for women and nonbinary people when we still have so far to go with one another? When we calcify the idea that we are *learned* and others are not, when in fact we're always learning?

You still don't have to be someone's friend just because you share their gender. And you don't have to love their work, either. But you can improve the climate of women's spaces, of professional events where we are present, by remembering how far you've come and how far you have to go. Pull wires, not hair. Build things together when you can and if you can. Be alone when you can. And check in with yourself on this every day: Remember who and what the real enemy is. It is never the other woman in the party with you.

SEXISM IN TECH
Katy Levinson

If you asked the most honest, insecure version of me for an answer about sexism in tech, I would probably reply "Please don't ask me," but I never say that, because I am a proud woman, and I don't want to be called a coward.

Nor is it that I don't care. I care a lot. I feel like I have to care, and I can't imagine any real way to escape it. These things are uncontroversially severe and unacceptable in our society, and we are point-blank not handling them.

On two occasions, my employers have offered me bribes to leave quietly because they were worried about sexual harassment claims either slightly before or after dramatic percentages of women either transferred to another department, quit, or were removed. I had not brought any harassment concerns forward prior to either offer. In both cases I have reason to believe I was the only woman offered financial compensation. I have spoken at a professional conference and had about two dozen drunk fully grown men shout-chant at me to take my shirt off, becoming louder and growing more numerous the longer nobody responded to them. Security did nothing, and I was on my own to de-escalate the situation.

I have been raped by a colleague—not just once, but several times over months. A second colleague at a different institution held me against a wall against my objections and struggles and hit me with objects for his own amusement. My female colleagues told me later that he raped some of them, and in much the same way my attacker had raped me. I've had a colleague scream at me that everything good I ever had was given to me because I was a girl and that if were a boy, nobody would even know my name. He screamed it in public to humiliate me. The worst part was that, as I told him to go fuck himself and tried not to cry, I couldn't prove to myself that what he said wasn't true. Nor could I prove it to myself later, lying awake in bed.

I have had interviewers attempt to solicit sexual favors from me mid-interview and discuss in significant detail precisely what they would like to do. All of these things have happened either in Silicon Valley working in tech, in an educational institution to get me there, or in a technical internship. The first incident happened when I was 14. Neither my rapist nor the man who hit me was at one of the places where I was offered a bribe.

Though others have surely seen worse and not all women have the same experience I do, I have seen things that nobody should have to put up with at work. I have seen these and a thousand others, some tiny, some giant. I'm not brave enough to write some of the things I have seen, because they are too easily traced back to individuals I don't want to pick a fight with. Saying there is sexism in tech is a very risky business, and walking around confidently with a "do your worst" attitude attracts those who would like to try.

There is one thing you know about every single person who has ever complained about an act of sexism loudly enough for the public to notice: they worry that they will be seen as liabilities for the rest of their career. No whistleblower has ever been given a "team player" award by the organization they spoke ill of. That shouldn't be too foreign a concept: people we call whistleblowers, who outed the wrongs of government or industry, certainly aren't doing it for personal gain. In this way, sexual harassment whistleblowing is the same as any other kind of whistleblowing.

Consider Mark Klein, who in 2006 blew the whistle on AT&T and the NSA for mass surveillance of Americans, or Thomas Andrews Drake who helped expose the NSA's Trailblazer project and was later charged under the Espionage Act. Despite doing the nation a service, neither of these men have been protected by the community they helped police. It is unlikely that anything a whistleblower on sexism in tech reveals will be nearly as clear cut, nor is the public likely to rally around them. Realistically, only bad things happen to the whistleblower. So when tries to discredit a whistleblower, ask yourself—what could the whistleblower's motive possibly be? They're knowingly ruining their own lives.

However, we don't call anybody who talks about sexism in tech a whistleblower. Even their staunchest allies don't call them that. We aren't that generous with words.

Nevertheless, any whistleblower on any topic risks everything, hoping they can prove both the actual wrongdoing, and that they aren't doing this for personal gain. People who don't believe you will consider you an enemy and call you "traitor" or "attention whore," but never whistleblower, and people who haven't bothered to research enough to form an opinion will call you a "liability."

Let's define some terms. I'll call the belief that the whistleblower is telling the truth "factual trust" and the belief that the whistleblower isn't doing this for personal gain "motivational trust." A person who has both factual and motivational trust in you is your ally (and you're theirs). A person who lacks either trust considers you an "enemy." Those who haven't made up their minds yet are normally waiting for more facts to be brought to them, but normally a topic loses communal interest long before the entire truth comes out. This means your claims are left as "unknown" and the community winds up leaving you forever marked as a "liability."

I'm not afraid of people who have made a real, rational effort to understand my position and still decided I am their enemy. I can't think of anything I could gain from this, and by not naming anybody, I'm making it clear

I'm not doing it for revenge. All that's left is the truth I'm bringing forward. Nothing is universally accepted, from a controversial issue like what health benefits organic food specifically provides, to something pretty widely accepted except by a select few, like the concept that we landed on the moon. Since all I'm claiming here is that sexism in tech is generally pervasive and toxic, my enemies have to believe that these things are physically impossible and consequently could not have happened to me. If there even exist people who believe such a thing, I don't care what they think of me because we won't work together well regardless. If these people are so pervasive that they're inescapable in tech, then I'll have to leave anyway, so I might as well find that out sooner than later.

What I fear instead is being labeled a liability. When somebody calls you a liability, it means they don't care whether you were doing something noble or just exploiting the system for personal gain. They just know there was some controversy around you. This is the horrible default bucket any woman who tries to speak up falls into, this terrible place where newspapers write things like "Employee Accuses Former Employer Of . . ."

Society hasn't examined the facts enough to really come to a conclusion, and so even in casual conversation people say things like "allegedly." Nobody wants to take a side and the story dies out in people's minds before the truth comes out. The impact on the would-be whistleblower is tremendous.

This is a terrible place to be if you can't immediately leave the freshly-kicked hornet's nest of an industry. Maybe you'll get threats of personal violence from those enemies, but they'll lose interest eventually. Scarier are those who either can't bother to research for themselves or were convinced by a well-researched enemy that you're a liability. People are going to pass you over for jobs because they think you might stir up trouble. Even if you aren't directly passed over, it counts in the other candidates' favor. To some degree, anybody who ever challenges the status quo accepts this, because humans are too lazy to check their facts. Altruism is required to make progress, but tech is a closely-knit network and being considered a liability has far-reaching consequences.

Some people think the personal gain is such a common motive they won't even check if their assumption makes sense. Those people are even scarier. They'll just assume you're a liability (or downright malicious) unless they spontaneously ingest overwhelming evidence you aren't. If everybody around you falls into this bucket, you've paid the price but not been heard. You're now blacklisted but without accomplishing change in the system. Before people can come forward and talk about their experiences of sexism in tech, they need to trust that this isn't going to happen to them. Otherwise they are either playing the odds with their employability or being self-destructive.

Honestly, I'm still dodging the question of sexism in tech. We already know rape is bad and that the long list of things I listed as "unquestionably unacceptable" are widely accepted to be, in fact, unquestionably unacceptable. It's even harder to talk about the things that could be questionably acceptable if you didn't have the backdrop of the far worse things which have happened, and which I believe happen fairly commonly to women in tech. I want to talk about the question more directly.

Did you know 4 percent of the men surveyed on an American college campus self-identified as rapists? As in, when asked if they had sex with somebody who either was in no position to say no or in the man's estimation was physically unable to say no, 4 percent of men said "yes." Half of those were repeat rapists, and those individuals averaged 5.8 victims. Similar results were found when surveying American armed forces. Why isn't that fact brought up at every discussion about professional equality? How are we to discuss the subtle ways that college-educated women are made to feel uncomfortable in the workplace if we can't discuss the very obvious ways college-aged women are made uncomfortable by being raped? How many times do we need to watch people discuss this as someone else's problem, instead of taking a serious look at our culture to see if it's here too?

This culture of avoidance is very prevalent in tech. In the last three years, I was asked not to use the words "sexism" or "racism" when speaking on a diversity panel because it might make the audience uncomfortable. The person who asked this had significant financial stake in the institution I worked for. Explaining that I was uncomfortable with that request was pretty hard.

Silicon Valley at least seems to understand that culture is important, but a lot of times when we talk about cultural power imbalances we default to a minimum standard of avoiding liability instead of actually handling problems. In fact, I'm not sure I have ever seen a sexual harassment seminar or mandatory-video-to-watch which strove to be anything more than plausible deniability fodder. Most seminars or videos seem to try to scare would-be harassers into not bringing liability on to the company. The companies want to avoid lawsuits at least as much, if not more, than they want to protect their female employees. I'm not sure it is any sort of improvement.

Here's a non-comprehensive litmus test for if your workplace equality efforts are working or not: do they try to give the impression that workplace inequality is "under control?" Everything I have read and seen says sexism is not under control in tech, and that it is in fact wildly out of control. Sexism in tech is not a thing to be kept "under control." It is the sort of thing that, when properly investigated, will fundamentally change the balance of power (in this case between genders), like any revelation a whistleblower brings forward would.

Your efforts to enable whistleblowers need to protect them, but also need to involve all the tools used in any response to other shocking revelations: investigation, fact finding and statistic-taking, and continued dedicated study. If your reactions to the issues of sexism in tech are crafted out of fear that a scandal will rock your safe place, if you only threaten punishments to your would-be harassing-employees and never educate them, point to a diversity hire, or point to a position you have created for this purpose and haven't touched in years, you are keeping the status quo rather than actually tackling our societal problems.

I had a boss once who knew he was sexist (also homophobic and transphobic), but was trying to get over it. He said some incredibly dumb things, like offering to have a company meeting at a strip club. He genuinely had bizarre concepts of what's appropriate and inappropriate behavior. He was ashamed of this and really trying to improve. Listening to him quote the sexual harassment seminars was the saddest bit: on one hand he was really trying, but on the other, everything he was quoting made absolutely no sense. I frequently found him putting so much effort in where it didn't really matter, like obsessively counting how many times he had asked a man vs a woman to carry heavy equipment. He always seemed overloaded with things to remember about "not being sexist" and afraid to get something wrong. It seemed almost heartless to risk getting him in trouble.

On the whole, however, I don't hold against him all the inappropriate things he did. The best I could do was kindly remind my boss when something made me uncomfortable, but he always looked panicked when I did. I didn't want to get him in trouble; in fact, half of my comments to him started with phrases like "you know people are going to take it the wrong way if they hear you saying that." I wish my male peers had helped him more in this regard. I feel they could have done it without making my boss feel like he was being directly threatened with a huge HR complaint. It's a real shame for our tech culture that there is no way to get somebody tutored about what is and isn't appropriate without also landing them in deep trouble.

Frankly, between the people who are mistreated because they are seen as persecutors, those who are seen as self-promoting, and those who are seen as liars, whistleblowing for sexism in tech is getting really unattractive for anybody who isn't willing to leave the tech industry. We're in a difficult place though because if we are asked and we deny that anything wrong went on, we know we'll just be trotted out as evidence against any actual whistleblower to show that nothing is wrong and they are just making stuff up. If we decline to comment, we're seen as cowards. It's not a pretty situation to be in.

What needs to change is three-fold.

The first thing is pretty simple: in all organizations, demand that there exists a code of conduct and clear method to report misconduct. Imagine right now that you have just witnessed something inappropriate in your workplace, at a conference or in a community. Do you have a place you could report it? Do you trust that it would be handled properly, or would they just try to avoid liability? Do you believe you would personally suffer for making such a report? If you're not comfortable with any of those answers, you have work to do. Reconsider what systems have been created, and fight for ones that treat this as a whistleblowing issue, not something to be "kept under control."

Second, while there will always be truly malicious people, most people just don't realize the harm of their action. There needs to be correction without punishment for people who are not malicious. With such a mechanism in place, people who see sexism in action can help fix it. At the same time, it allows those who are doing things wrong to learn in a safe environment. For more about this approach, check out some of the great articles about call-in culture. The goal is simple here: help your well-intentioned friends figure out they are hurting people without making it seem like a threat or shaming. It's easiest for you if you aren't the one being wronged. This step is important because whistleblowers need allies, and we need people to not be afraid of announcing they are allies. This means two things: One, that we be welcoming and patient with those striving to be better, and two, that our allies (and those of us trying to lead the charge) be committed to self-improvement whenever the opportunity presents itself.

Third, and most important, is making a serious personal commitment to solving this. You're tired of hearing about this "women in tech" stuff, and we're tired of living it, but there are some big issues here, and we're not going to solve them by pretending they don't exist because we're bored or afraid of them. We need serious discussions, and we have to have educated opinions about what's wrong and how to fix it. We need to mull these ideas around until we come to some combination of hard data and cultural consensus before we can get meaningful change.

Making a personal commitment means forming an opinion on more than just the broad concepts. It also requires learning about specific instances of harassment. Spend enough time reading material from both sides to develop a well-informed opinion, or be honest about not knowing enough. Don't defend an opinion that isn't well thought through. Then, use that opinion to make sure whistleblowing is taken seriously. When we fail to engage whistleblowing in our own lives or in institutions we deal with, we're hanging the whistleblowers out to dry. At best, we allow them to be marked as "liabilities"; at worst, we leave them to suffer at the hands of their enemies.

For clarity, I'm going to now state my three specific requests:

Make sure the systems to handle malicious abuses of power against women have teeth, and that they seek to let the disenfranchised blow the whistle, rather than simply "keeping stuff under control."

Help your well-intentioned peers who are still making mistakes do better without threatening them or humiliating them.

Make a public commitment to taking potential whistleblowers seriously. Commit to educating yourself, to having an opinion, and, if you believe the whistleblower's claims might have merit, to helping. Live up to that commitment.

#Whistleblower hashtags are cute, but I'd prefer we get some meaningful, lasting change. I hope we decide we are ready to listen with the sort of radical honesty that will make change possible. I hope we're ready to commit to spending the time helping our culture figure this out, so that people who care won't be left looking like liabilities. Above all, I hope we're ready to promise people that talking about this is worth the risk, and then to make good on that promise. I want us to promise that if we see something wrong we'll say something instead of looking away again and leaving the would-be whistleblower vulnerable.

I chose not to make this a personal piece, because the message is universal. Still, I can't help adding one personal note, if you'll bear with me:

> If you're not ready to make a commitment to being part of the solution, don't ask me to speak publicly about sexism in tech. It's not that I'm scared (though I am), it's because you'll be asking me to take a serious professional risk for no purpose at all.

THAT'S IT—I'M FINISHED DEFENDING SEXISM IN TECH

Elissa Shevinsky

I thought that we didn't need more women in tech. I was wrong.

What's troubling is that I should have known better. I spent the last year building female-centric dating apps. In March, I was awarded "today's winner of the app designed for the ladies without being too patronizing about it" by Jezebel. It was clear to me that the biggest problem with online dating was that most dating apps are designed by men. But I saw this as a problem unique to my little corner of the tech world.

I cared about my gynecologist being a woman. But I didn't care if the software that I use daily was written by a woman or a dude. Why would that matter? After yesterday's antics at the TechCrunch Disrupt

Hackathon, I have to admit that I was wrong. Gender matters.

Yesterday's TechCrunch Disrupt Hackathon presentations debuted with Titstare. The two Australians behind the weekend hack were given 60 seconds to pitch their app. They opened with, "Titstare is an app where you take photos of yourself staring at tits" and closed their presentation saying, "It's the breast, most titillating fun you can't have."

The juvenile performances didn't end there. The demo for "Circle Shake"—hosted at SoTopless.com—featured groaning and fake masturbation, while the hacker shook his phone up and down as fast as he could.

If there was one tweet that summed up "Titstare" at the TC Disrupt Hackathon, it was this:

KIM @KKJORDAN
Titstare guys got a very loud applause from audience. Thank god sexism isn't alive and well in the tech sector. SO PROUD TO HAVE MY KID HERE

To its credit, TechCrunch responded quickly to Titshare, noting the following change in policy: "Every presentation is getting a thorough screening from this hackathon onward. Any type of sexism or other discriminatory and/or derogatory speech will not be allowed."

What's worse is this kind of BS is pervasive enough that incidents occur with regularity at industry events, and not all hosts are as quick to respond as TechCrunch.

Similar accusations were levied at DefCon. DefCon is troubling because the sexist content is part of official programming. DefCon's "Hacker Jeopardy" features a woman undressing and has been called out as "misogynistic bullshit."

DefCon founder Jeff Moss has defended Hacker Jeopardy, noting that the strip act performed by "Vinyl Vanna" has historically been a part of Hacker Jeopardy. Moss elaborated by distinguishing between "sexy" and "sexism."

I had defended DefCon's right to do whatever they want. I had suggested on Twitter that Women 2.0 and the Hacker Dojo start an alternative security conference. I was wrong. I take this back. We shouldn't have to. Seeing Titstare steal the show at the TC Disrupt Hackathon was an epiphany for me. Reasonable, professional, and non-sexist behavior should be an industry standard.

I finally have to admit that pervasive brogramming and its inherent sexism is a problem. Nine year old Alexandra Jordan presented the hack "superfunkidtime .com" on stage and our biggest take-away from the Disrupt Hackathon is that some jackasses presented an app about boobs? Sexism is such a big distraction that it's worth taking head on, and dismantling.

I posted my new position on Twitter, and now find myself explaining why I ever thought sexism in tech was OK.

ELISSA SHEVINSKY @ELISSABETH
I'm now of the opinion that pervasive bro-ness is enough of a distraction to be worth dismantling. @rachelsklar @GirlsWhoCode @shanley @DBNess

RACHELSKLAR @RACHELSKLAR
@ElissaBeth @GirlsWhoCode @shanley @DBNess Why was that ever your position?!

I'd also been in tech since 2001. I wasn't seeing the problems clearly because I'd been part of the industry for too long. I also wanted to focus on getting things done rather than on feminist-inspired activism. So I made the bros-only atmosphere work for me. I overcompensated by picking a frat boy to cofound a company with me (he was MIT & YC, by the way). I had the greatest time drinking Scotch at Google I/O with some of the best CTOs in the media industry. They treated me like a bro. I didn't want to lose those moments. And I thought that there was room for other women to have a similarly good experience.

I experienced sexism all the time, but I overlooked it because I was too busy working. My year living and working with younger Silicon Valley startup guys in the SoMA district of San Francisco was an onslaught of misogyny, penis jokes, porn references, and general lack of common courtesy. The oddest part was the inability to switch gears. What made these guys think that I'd want to hear their masturbation humor? That's what happened at the Disrupt hackathon. Those guys weren't able to switch gears out of brogrammer mode. One wonders if they ever switch gears.

Let's be clear—sexism isn't owned by startup bros from frats out of MIT. I've been hit on by VCs (one messaged me on Gchat to ask if my OKCupid profile was for research) and another introduced himself at the TC August Capital party by stating that he'd like to make out with me (to be fair, my badge read "CEO of MakeOut Labs," but that introduction was brazen). I've been sympathetic to these bad actors. With so few women around, it's almost reasonable that they can't get past seeing me as one of their only romantic prospects. And yet, we find ourselves wondering why more women don't choose to be part of this world.

Despite all of this, I continued to defend the status quo. I wanted to just drink Scotch with my guy friends and build software. I'm done now. I didn't want to think about gender issues but the alternative is tit and dick jokes at our industry's most respected events.

Proactively enforcing standards at major tech events is a good start. But we need to address the root cause as well. Hackers at these events shouldn't be trying to present apps like Titstare as demonstrations. Parents should feel comfortable bringing their nine-year-olds to these events. Making tech hospitable to women won't be easy but this much is clear: we do need to figure out how to get more women in the room.

The controversy over "Titstare" set off a wave of feminist activism (and institutional changes at tech companies and VC firms) that dramatically improved the Silicon Valley ecosystem. I look back to what tech culture was like in 2012, and it's a different beast now. Things are better. I am relieved.

But better is not the same as good.

I remain deeply troubled by the lack of respect shown by men in spaces that are meant to be professional. There is, at times, an unwillingness to show consideration for people who do not appreciate locker room humor or sexism/racism at community events. I expect speakers at prestigious events to show respect. I expect managers and coworkers to follow basic norms for professionalism. I continue to be disappointed.

I was a speaker at GirlDevWeek, which gave me access to the speaker's lounge for Developer Week. I overheard a man who gives frequent talks about programming, as he discussed his spontaneous speaking style. He explained that he has to be himself when he gives talks, and that he sometimes curses or uses offensive language. He was aware that he offended his audience, regularly, but said "I gotta be in the moment. I gotta be me."

Startups and tech culture have long been a space where boys could be boys. And there are some boys—grown boys—who are fighting to keep it this way. The struggle for cultural control is messy and we are smack in the middle of it.

Consider TechCrunch's 2015 awards show "The Crunchies." TechCrunch's editorial board is run by women and feminists and people who are vigilant about appropriate behavior at their events. Since the incidents at TechCrunch Disrupt in 2013, TechCrunch has implemented solid policies for conferences inspired by the awesome people at 'Geek Feminism." Their (recently implemented) "anti-harassment' policy includes the following language as of March 2015:

"We will not and do not tolerate harassment of conference participants in any form including overly sexualized or demeaning comments during talks or anything that threatens personal safety. Conference participants violating these rules may be sanctioned or expelled from the conference without a refund at the discretion of the conference organizers."

Despite this, speaker TJ Miller gave an increasingly drunken—and demeaning—performance at "The Crunchies." Miller called audience member Gabi Holzwarth a bitch three times and managed to insult Asians, all in the span of one sentence. This behavior escalated through the course of the evening. I walked out of the show, joined by other not-amused party-goers, before it was over.

In a widely read post on Medium, Twitter executive Katie Stanton (who was there to accept Twitter's award) wrote "I left as soon as I received the Crunchie, saddened and disappointed to see such a public lack of respect for women."

This happened despite a mixed-gender audience and clearly set guidelines for TechCrunch speakers. Just like the speaker that I had overheard at DevWeek, TJ Miller didn't really care about community guidelines or who was in his audience.

My essay in response to "Titstare" was very honest. I hadn't given much thought to feminism before "Titstare" and this was the start of my thought process about how to make things better. My initial conclusion—that all we need is to get more women in the room—was naïve. As magical as femininity may be, it is not the cure-all for this cultural conflict.

Having women in the audience doesn't turn inconsiderate speakers into nice ones. And having women in the office doesn't turn hostile environments into respectful ones, at least not overnight. And in the meantime, those women are now subject to experiencing whatever problems we were hoping they would solve.

It's wrong to ask women to come in and be the fix— because women are not the problem.

We also need men to step up and to welcome us.

The good news is that's starting to happen. The major institutions in Silicon Valley are finally saying that they value gender balance. Silicon Valley is a far better place now than it was when I lived with frat boy programmers in 2012. But as the stories in this anthology illustrate, we can do a lot better. And we should.

FICTIVE ETHNICITY AND NERDS

Katherine Cross

Once tormented by jocks and "normal" kids, (male) nerds are now on the top of the social food chain. Yet such nerds still see themselves as marginalized; defensive. It takes time to realize one's changed social status, and the responsibilities that come with leadership. In ascending to a place of social dominance, without an accompanying egalitarianism or noblesse oblige, have nerds become the new schoolyard bullies?

When young men tell you that they have found love, community, and even family among those technical tribes known as gamers, nerds, and geeks, you should believe them.

Though the phrase "boys' club" is on everyone's lips these days when talking about sexist power dynamics in technology, less attention is paid to the strong and weak nuclear forces that hold that club together. Gender (and race) are part of the formula, but those identities that constellate around the simulacrum of "nerd," so beloved of filmmakers and marketers alike, are even more important in terms of defining who's in, who's out, and why.

It is what gives "the club" in technology its shape and purpose. The mythology of the nerd—the much beleaguered, aggressively bullied, unloved young (usually white) men whose brilliance was never appreciated by their peers, but who ultimately triumphed—is writ in the stars of the technology world today, leaving us all in the thrall of an epic retelling of *Revenge of the Nerds*, with each of us playing an unwilling part in a high school drama that never quite stopped.

I.

The Boys' Club in tech does not simply admit any "boy," but rather, depends on its members all being true believers in some version of this mythology. The key components of the myth: the bullying, the sense of being discriminated against because of one's hobbies, smarts, or interests, the implicit sense that being a nerd represented a superior form of manhood to its "jock" or openly macho counterpart, that it always entailed rejection by women for sex and companionship, and that one's intellect entitled one to rule the roost of adulthood, all congeal into a nomos, a meaningful order, in the various precincts of tech culture that acts as a canopy of meaning for us all.

"Nomos" in the sense I'm using it owes itself to sociologist Peter L. Berger's 1967 study The Sacred Canopy. To summarize briefly, "nomos" is, as I said, a meaningful order; it synthesizes meanings into a coherent system of beliefs that provides people in a given society with a common schema with which to approach the world. Think of it as the filter through which one interprets everything they see; a heuristic device through which one knows the world. I like Berger's term because it's deliberately meant as a sort of sociological counterpart to "cosmos," and functions as a good metaphor for the taken-for-granted world of a given society.

In this way, a nomos describes a whole system of ideas, beliefs, mores, and folkways for a given community, and for many in the tech universe, to be part of the tribe of "nerd" generally presupposes some core nomic ideas about history and shared identity.

The triumph of the nerd is a gendered one; however many of us as women, LGBT/queer people, or people of color might have experienced bullying (and actual discrimination atop it), the vision of who gets to be a nerd, a geek, or a gamer, remains defined by a classic image that is now plastered on bus shelters nationwide of the *Big Bang Theory*-style pretentious, perpetually adolescent, young male nerds.

Yet it's more than just being a man. This string of identities is about a rather distinct sense of masculinity with a few core qualifications, what sociologist Raewyn Connell once called "the masculinity of the counting house" defined by technical mastery as opposed to the "conquistador"-style manhood characterized by aggression and violent displays of strength.

In addition, these identities as they are now often employed, constitute a "fictive ethnicity," to borrow a term from games scholar Celia Pearce, an "identity adopted around an imaginary homeland." That homeland, its culture, its myths, its nomos, are what make up the "boys club" and what make it so enduring and seemingly impenetrable.

II.

Meritocracy, or at least the unquestioned conviction in its status as a law of the universe, is endemic to Silicon Valley and its environs. Much of that can be said to come from not only an economic ideology—that is, one which reifies the much older Horatio Alger legend and its attendant bootstrap-based thinking—but also from the sense that being a technologist and having the skills required to be one is an affirmative elective identity. You choose to be a nerd, in a way that one does not choose to be one's race or gender. In theory, then, this means that being a nerd/geek/gamer is open to everyone who has the technical know-how to master the skills required.

All can apply to join this tribe of formerly bullied and derided social outcasts in order to pool knowledge and resources to make a better world for those who once despised them. That one chooses to be part of this group is essential to its sense of identity; like building a more efficient computer, being a nerd is often seen to be about building a better identity, a better community that improves on the old ascribed identities of the past that seem to cause so much political strife.

It's Identity 2.0.

This is, by no means, to suggest that "nerd" identity (or "geek" or "gamer") is monolithic. There are competing ideas for just what each of these identities mean, some slightly more inclusive than others. But there are, as I suggested earlier, some core features.

History: this is, perhaps, the brightest constellation in the nomos of nerd identity. The shared "territory" described earlier can include physical spaces—offices, labs, chatrooms, gaming guilds/clans—but it also includes psychic ones like a sense of universal history, one shared by all nerds. MIT professor Scott Aaronson wrote a controversial and personally-searching comment on his own blog that was widely reported on, pushing back against the idea that "enlightened" men in technology and STEM fields were uniquely sexist, describing instead a long childhood history where he felt bullied by other boys for being a nerd, and ostracized by girls who denied him sexual companionship for the same reason, as well as feeling constantly villainized for being male.

He writes: "Here's the thing: I spent my formative years—basically, from the age of 12 until my mid-20s—feeling not 'entitled,' not 'privileged,' but terrified. I was

terrified that one of my female classmates would somehow find out that I sexually desired her, and that the
instant she did, I would be scorned, laughed at, called a
creep and a weirdo, maybe even expelled from school or
sent to prison."

This is a history that is, obviously, based on real
events. Bullying is a pandemic in our schools, and it
remains popular to bully "teacher's pets" and nerds specifically. But the meaning ascribed to all this—especially
the stark gendering Aaronson applies here—is what is
distinct, what transforms these memories from events
into history. A shared history of having been bullied by
boys and denied by girls, hated for being a nerd, and,
particularly, a hidden social outcast whose experience
with prejudice was on a par with actual ethnic and sexual
minorities.

In similar communities, like those of gaming, this
sense of shared history includes a collective memory of
bruising censorship wars in the 90s and early 2000s, a
sense that their beloved hobby was under attack from
all sides and that "gamers" had to defend it from the
grasping hands of the censor, whether they were parents,
priests, or politicians.

Superior Masculinity: Aaronson's comment also
contains another useful element often essential to this
mentality: the sense that nerds are doing manhood in
a unique and special way that is not only better than
competing masculinities, but is unfairly slighted and not
fully recognized for its superiority, especially by women.

Aaronson should be quoted in full here: "The same girls who I was terrified would pepper-spray me and call the police if I looked in their direction, often responded to the crudest advances of the most Neanderthal of men by accepting those advances . . . Yet it was I, the nerd, and not the Neanderthals, who needed to check his privilege and examine his hidden entitlement!"

This is where we return to Connell's distinction between conquistador masculinity (or "Neanderthal" as Aaronson puts it) and the masculinity of the counting house. Manhood based on technical mastery, one's intellect and mental acuity, rather than on physical strength was imagined to be superior, and latter-day nerd identity is the most recent reification of this kind of masculinity. Nerds are better, worthier kinds of men, in this conception because they are clever and not physically violent.

When combined with other tropes of nerd culture—certain hobbies and interests, mastery and control of technologies that are often changing the world for the better, "geek chic" fashion, a sense of being uniquely socially liberal and tolerant—we get the sense of Identity 2.0 discussed earlier.

High School Springs Eternal: The stereotypical social tropes of a suburban high school—jocks and cheerleaders on one side, nerdy boys on the other—remain the ideal way to interpret and understand the social world for plenty of adults who hew to nerd identities. But to fully explain how this works, we shall have to bring real women, not just the mythic romantic rejectors of ages past, into the discussion.

III.

Throughout this essay we have spoken of "nerds" as if they are all or implicitly all male; this was in service to illustrating the popular conception of this group, however, and, particularly, an implicit self-conception among many men in the tech industry.

Plenty of women could be said to be nerds, geeks, and gamers—myself enthusiastically included, as it happens. But this fictive ethnicity is not made for us, in a variety of ways. The shared history that is a part of the nerd nomos, for instance, strongly implies a male referent. Girls and women were always Other, adorning the arms of the "Neanderthals," looking down their noses at dorky boys, and ready to blow a rape whistle at the drop of a hat.

I was bullied quite viciously as a child because I was a nerd—the shy teacher's pet who didn't realize that publicly and proudly saying she loved Bill Nye The Science Guy was a one-way ticket to being bullied. In seventh grade I was body-slammed on the hardwood floor of my school's gym so hard that to this day my right leg occasionally suffers shooting pains, particularly around my hip and femur.

I felt it aching as I read Professor Aaronson's commentary, indeed.

This complicating history of women—cis, trans, POC, and LGBT nerds—is not part of the dominant nomos because the key symbolism makes no room for us. The story of the awkward bespectacled nerd girl who was passed over for prom even by the geeky boys never gets to be part of this shared history because it's the round peg in the square hole of masculine tales like Aaronson's.

What's more, women's role in nerd cosmology is that of the perpetual snobbish, mocking cheerleader. This inflects male nerds' perception of feminism in interesting ways. Aaronson's comment was written in reply to a feminist, after all, who had been arguing that sexism was a particular problem in STEM fields and tech culture. To many of these men, even those like Aaronson himself who identify as feminists and egalitarians, it is all too easy to subconsciously confound women who say "this is sexist" with the young girls who said (or were believed to have said) "you're gross and a creep and I'll never date you."

Indeed, feminist media critic Anita Sarkeesian was likened to a prom queen by some gamers resentful of her feminist critiques of sexist elements in video games, and one person accused her of metaphorically "stuffing them in a locker."

Such ideas only make sense in the nomos of nerd identity, and it's visions like this which leave women passively excluded, even by men who are quite sincere in their egalitarian convictions. They inhabit a psychic territory that depends on a gendered pageant that women and minorities did not consent to.

In this way, "nerd" becomes a fictive ethnicity premised on that territory. To the limited extent women and minorities may be fully welcomed into it, it is contingent on us checking all other identities in at the door, so to speak. So long as one reifies the male-centered history and culture of nerd identity, one will find a measure of acceptance.

Gaming makes for a useful case study here as it exists at a unique collision of professional nerd identities in the technology industry (developers, designers, coders, etc.) and fans, the gamers themselves, modders, fan artists, amateur coders, and so forth. Women, as well as racial and sexual minorities, find a contingent acceptance in this space so long as they do not challenge the core narratives of the fictive ethnicity: that it is meritocratic, that (male) nerds were bullied and overcame it by joining this affinity group of gamers, that one must be forever on the lookout for "censors"—be they Christian conservatives or feminists—and that gamers are smarter, better people who are more tolerant than other male-dominated groups because they are clever.

If you accept all that at face-value, make it an article of one's creed, and avoid "making an issue" of one's identity as, say, a transgender woman, or a person of color, then you'll find a contingent form of acceptance within the fictive ethnicity. Put simply, "nerd" must be your first and last identity. Identity 2.0 brooks none of the old 1.0 identities that (white male) nerds believe to only cause dissension.

This is part of what creates a consistent canopy of meaning. Some gamers pass around snarky infographic timelines that posit that "women" only became interested in games sometime around 2005–6 and that all was harmonious before then. Again and again, feminist women are attacked because we were believed to be the snooty popular girls picking on them in high school for being gaming nerds, and who are now neophytes storming in to ruin their hobby. It cannot be admitted that we might have been gaming during our childhoods as well. This is part of the mythology that a number of male gamers accept as a factual reading of their history. The legend of past harmony disturbed by a latter-day invasion of "girl gamers" and feminists is central—and this is specifically a shared vision, something outsiders did to a cohesive and identifiable group called "gamers." Some others adopt a different but compatible route which highlights the work of women developers, in a bid to assert another core myth, that the gaming community is uniquely tolerant and diverse. But both myths work together to support the same idea: anyone complaining about prejudice in gaming spaces is an outsider who does not grasp the culture and is apt to take something away from it, or even destroy it. This has a great deal of homology with other precincts of tech culture.

IV.

For lonely, isolated, dejected men who had a history of being ostracized for their talents and hobbies, these fictive ethnicities provide an island of safety and reprieve, a world somewhere over the hills of high school that promises community and family. It makes the thing they were hurt for (the appellation of being a "nerd") something to take pride in, a form of counter-recognition that vivifies their sense of importance and talent, stemming from the very same reasons people picked on them in the first place. Their hobbies and skills, which once led to them being targeted for abuse, could now be markers of an affirmative identity of cool game-changing lords of technology who would both save and inherit the Earth.

It is hard not to see the appeal of this, naturally. Even when it manifests in more toxic ways, as it did with the GamerGate movement of 2014, which centered on an amplified version of this form of nerd/gamer identity that was even more exclusionary and more riven by aggrieved entitlement; these self-identified gamers saw not just their fictive territory, but their very existence as being under attack, as if feminists literally wanted to extermi-nate everything that they were. This conviction, in turn, justified the long running waves of harassment and attack against female gaming critics, journalists, developers and their male allies for months on end—some of which, as of this writing, have yet to end, all in the name of thwarting this fictional invasion that is increasingly used to solidify a coherent sense of gamer identity.

The "Other" against which so many of these nerd identities are defined is gendered and raced. From "whiny" queer gamers to "invading" feminist women to "Chinese gold farmers," threats come from all angles, casting long shadows from the fragile borders of this identity. Nerds, including self-identified ones, come from all backgrounds comprising a diverse spectrum of humanity, but we do not all stand equally beneath that nomic canopy, much to the detriment of everyone involved. So much of the fictive ethnicity of nerd is based on ideas that, by their very nature and in their retellings, place women and minorities in impossible positions.

But this mentality—that all nerds, geeks, and gamers have a shared identity and culture—also gives license to all manner of toxic behaviours, not least an alarming number of adults who seem determined to avenge their childhood traumas through their identity, making of nerd culture the very opposite of what it is intended to be—a spiny-shelled, defensive, fragile self, which is defined by perpetual attack. Any nerd who does not identify as a white man is interpreted as a threatening outsider who will pillage it all—be it freewheeling Silicon Valley disruption culture, to gaming's T&A-focused excesses. That is the nature of the "boys' club" as it stands in tech; banded together not just by gender, but by ideology and an identity that feeds on ongoing inequalities.

Identity evolves naturally, but if we must have an identity 2.0 in the here and now—a consciously-constructed, distributed network of geeky and technically talented people—we'd do well to start patching it right now.

NOTES FROM A GAME INDUSTRY OUTCAST
Squinky

Making something that people love is hard. So is building a company. And we talk about that endlessly in the start-up scene. This has always frustrated me. Not because it's not true, but because it hasn't been the hardest part of start-ups for me. The hardest part has been fitting in. "Cultural fit," as we say.

Hi, I'm Squinky and I used to think I wanted nothing more in life than to be a professional game designer. I was about ten years old when I got clued in that making videogames was something you could actually do as a career. I was playing Full Throttle, an adventure game by LucasArts, and my younger brother had gotten the strategy guide from a friend. I would read it, fascinated, even after finishing the game itself. What I remember best was that the last chapter of the strategy guide contained short biographies of every person who worked on the game. From that point on, I did everything I could to follow in the footsteps of these much-admired people who got to make games for a living. I dabbled in hobbyist game development as a teen and later went to university for a computer science degree.

The first game I ever made was a LucasArts-style point-and-click adventure game called Cubert Badbone, P.I. I started working on it when I was 13 and finished it when I was 16. The supporting cast was filled with ridiculous, over-the-top aliens and proto-queer human characters loosely based on me and my friends, but the main character was a male noir detective archetype.

Why would I make the protagonist of my game a clone of every other straight white man in fiction? I thought that was how I was supposed to write stories. Every noir detective I read in a book, watched on a screen, or played in a game was a straight white man. It didn't occur to me to change that in my own work.

In 2006, I got my big break as an intern at Telltale Games. I actually got to work with a few of the people whose names I recognized from the Full Throttle strategy guide! Two years later, upon graduating from school, I would go on to work at another company on a project with Ron Gilbert, best known as the creator of LucasArts's Monkey Island series. For those readers who aren't in indie games, these are some of the gaming industry's luminaries.

That's a pretty impressive origin story, I know. I had a lot of privilege in getting this far. I grew up in Canada, upper middle class enough to have a computer in the house (and enough time to play with it). I was able to afford a university education. But a lot was stacked against me in other ways. I'm of mixed-race in a predominantly white society. I was assigned female at birth and raised as a girl, but that never felt quite right. As if that wasn't enough, I was socially awkward and introverted in a community where being outgoing and gregarious is important. As a nerdy, bookish, creative child I'd longed for a place where I would belong. I'd dreamed that gaming would be that place. But, as you can imagine, the game industry didn't actually want me in it.

In the beginning, I felt very welcome. Everyone was impressed by how much I'd accomplished at such a young age. I noticed straight away that there was a shortage of non-white non-men in games, and that I was often the odd one out, but I thought it meant that I was special. That my differences wouldn't hinder me from going on to Do Great Things.

The gaming industry is a business, first and foremost. As it turned out, gaming studios like Telltale Games only wanted me insofar as my youth and passion helped them make money by providing them with cheap labor. When my passion extended toward a desire for positive social change that didn't directly further the ideals of marketers and producers, suddenly I became a liability.

A lot of people care about diversity insofar as it makes money. When I used to go to industry events, a lot of people would talk about, say, designing games for women in terms of them being an untapped market, and this felt very strange and superficial to me. No one ever talked about any of the intrinsic, psychological benefits of representing marginalized people in games, or about how it simply is a good thing to do. It was all about the money. And yes, we all gotta eat, but making it only about money was still really alienating.

As if being a genderqueer person of color in an industry of white men wasn't alienating enough.

I was ignored and dismissed by industry people—and still am, actually. I'm not really someone you can stereotype or place, so most people would rather pretend I don't exist than try to fit me into a category. My identity is a kind of invisibility cloak.

A little more than a decade after Cubert Badbone, I released another noir detective adventure game called Dominique Pamplemousse in "It's All Over Once The Fat Lady Sings!" It is, currently, the work for which I'm best known.

Revisiting the noir detective adventure game genre came differently to me this time around. For one thing, I decided to turn the entire game into a musical—the kind where every character frequently bursts into song. I also hand-made all the art using claymation characters and other household objects. Finally, the main character, Dominique, was neither male nor female, but genderqueer, like me.

My own "coming out as genderqueer" process just so happened to coincide, gradually, with my writing of Dominique Pamplemousse, to the point that by the time the game was released, there was no hiding anymore. The game gave me the starting point I needed to explain to people that I prefer to be called "Squinky" and that I use singular they pronouns. Over the next year, as DomPam grew in exposure, first from being selected for IndieCade, then from being nominated for four awards at the Independent Games Festival, I became more visible than I'd ever been before.

I'd been waiting and hoping for something like this, some kind of critical recognition, to happen for ages, but now that it had, I wasn't sure how I felt about it. The night of the Independent Games Festival, I didn't actually win any of the four awards I was nominated for. I was disappointed, sure—I could definitely have used some of that prize money—but in a big way, I was relieved.

Today, more than ever, visibility for marginalized people in games is an occupational hazard. It was hard enough being perceived as a Woman In Games, but now that I'm a Genderqueer Person In Games, it's become even more complicated. While many of my professional acquaintances and colleagues respect my identity and at least attempt to use the correct pronouns, every Internet article written about me is filled with anonymous randos in the comments section misgendering me, misinterpreting my carefully chosen words, and in the worst cases, making creepy, disgusting remarks about my physical appearance. The Steam page for Dominique Pample-mousse is filled with vitriolic negative reviews, berating it for not looking or sounding like what a game is supposed to look and sound like.

While it's true that I don't even get anywhere close to the volume of harassment directed at Anita Sarkeesian or Zoe Quinn—both of whom I deeply admire and even have the pleasure of knowing in person—the pervasive fear exists that one day I'll get too popular for my own good, that I'll make one misstep or anger the wrong person and have the same cruel fate bestowed upon me.

For now, I'm still here, creating games more or less free from the shackles of the commercial game industry. My work has been enjoyed by artists, writers, readers, musicians, grad students, professors, parents, kids, and many others who don't fit the stereotype many people think of when they hear the word "gamer." That's meaningful.

MAKING GAMES IS EASY, BELONGING IS HARD
Squinky

Squinky's second piece in this collection, "Making Games is Easy, Belonging is Hard" was first delivered as a speech by Squinky—to a standing ovation—at the Game Developers Conference in 2014.

Making games is easy. Belonging is hard.

My game, Dominique Pamplemousse in "It's All Over Once The Fat Lady Sings!" was nominated for four Independent Games Festival awards. I didn't actually win anything, but instead of being disappointed like a normal person would be, I felt relieved.

Who feels relieved to lose? I mean, seriously.

The thing is, being recognized for awards like the IGF means being seen. And being seen, when you're a person who looks like me, is a double-edged sword.

The more attention and notoriety I get, the more I start wondering when all the 4Chan trolls are going to come out and get me. Like they've done to, oh, pretty much every single person I like and respect in games.

I've already started to see them pop up on Steam. I know they're just trolls, and I'm just supposed to ignore them. But honestly? I'm terrified.

Maybe it's better to be invisible. I know invisible. I can live with invisible.

My name is Deirdra Kiai. It was given to me by my parents, and I like it because no one else has it. It's memorable. It's a name that makes you stop and go, wait, how do you spell that? It's a product of the great big mix of cultures in which I was brought up. It's a name that says so much about who I am and where I come from.

My friends, however, call me Squinky. I firmly believe that everyone should have the opportunity to pick a name of their own choosing, and I found Squinky when I played The Secret of Monkey Island as an impressionable pre-teen. Somehow, it just fits. It's cute. It's gender-neutral. And being born with a name like Deirdra Kiai is, in many ways, a lot like being named Guybrush Threepwood [the hero of The Secret of Monkey Island].

It's also worth mentioning that Monkey Island was the game that first made me understand the potential of games as a way to tell stories. While I'd already been making art on computers ever since discovering MS Paint at age three, it was after playing Monkey Island that I was like, yes, this is the thing I want to be doing with my life.

And that's exactly what I've done. I released my first completed game in high school. I got an industry job right out of undergrad working on a game with Ron Gilbert, the guy who created Monkey Island. If anyone was a great fit for the game industry, it was me. Except, the truth is, I wasn't. I'm not. I don't think I ever will be.

Making games is easy. Belonging is hard.

Okay, if you've ever made a game before, you know it isn't really easy. But compare that to not fitting in, not being one of the guys, AND not being one of the gals either . . . well, I could make a million games with the energy that trying to belong takes out of me. I hate how people who aren't straight white cisgender men are treated in the game industry. I hate that so many women can't come to a professional event without getting hit on by some creepy dude . . . and I hate that it never, ever happens to me. I mean, who even thinks this? Shouldn't I feel happy that I'm not getting hit on? No, I feel like shit. I start to wonder, what's wrong with me? I clearly don't look manly or bearded or stubbly enough, so I don't get to be treated like a real human, but I'm also not hot enough for any of their creepy attention. I'm like invisible or something.

And it's not just true of me; it's true of all manner of us who don't fit a certain young, thin, white, femme, able-bodied heteropatriarchal beauty standard.

The double bind of, if you're hot enough, you get to have your hard-earned accomplishments diminished, and if you're not hot enough . . . well, you're defective.

Disgusting. Completely irrelevant. Heads, they win, tails, you lose.

Making games is easy. Belonging is hard.

I've always had the sense that people can't quite place me. I make people uncomfortable because I don't fit neatly into a demographic. Marketing departments don't just completely ignore me, they don't even believe I exist.

Like any other media, games were never meant for people like me. They were always someone else's story. And because of that, all I worked on were other people's stories, too. I couldn't make games about myself because I didn't even know who I was. How could I? I never saw myself represented anywhere, so how could I even see myself at all?

Making games is easy. Belonging is hard.

I learned to push and shove my way in, because I was afraid that if I didn't, I would disappear. I became one of those outspoken angry feminists everyone loves to hate, daring to say out loud all the things everyone else was silent about, because they didn't want to burn any professional bridges. The one they always privately claimed they agreed with, except, you know, we still want to be marketable to gamers.

I became their scapegoat. I was willing. I was young, foolish, and had nothing to lose.

I didn't last in the industry very long, as you can probably imagine. I was pushed over to the margins, where I quietly worked alone on my own projects, desperately struggling to find my voice.

They could exclude me all they wanted, but they couldn't stop me from making games. When I was twenty-five, I started playing a browser-based RPG called Echo Bazaar, which has since been renamed to Fallen London. As I created my character, I discovered that, along with the standard "man" and "woman" options, I could also choose to be a "person of mysterious and indistinct gender".

When I realized that choosing that third option felt more right than anything, that I didn't have to be a defective woman or a defective man but just myself . . . something inside me just unlocked. Slowly but surely, I started to dress and present differently, so that when I looked in the mirror, I started to see someone who looked more like how I felt.

I started to embrace the use of singular they. Who cares if it's grammatically incorrect? And all these feelings that were bubbling up got poured into a game of my own, a game in which I vented my frustrations with binary categories, my desire to be seen as a person, not a stereotype . . . and that game later went on to be nominated for four IGF awards.

And now I'm here.

But the truth is, I don't think anyone can fully be described by a gender or a race or a sexuality or any other limiting category. I think there are as many target audiences as there are people.

One day, I want to see a game industry that understands this. I want to see a game industry that tells its young and up-and-coming developers that their stories are valuable, that their unique creative voices are worth cultivating. I want to see a game industry where people are still making games when they're old. I want it to be okay to make things that are authentic and true and weird. No—not just okay, but important.   .

I've been able to do these things, but only in spite of the industry's social pressure not to. Imagine what I could have done if I'd been encouraged instead of ignored. Imagine how many other brilliant, talented people could be making weird, wonderful games along with me.

Last year, I was at anna anthropy's reading of Cara Ellison's poem, "Romero's Wives," at the rant panel, and suddenly, I started crying. Not just tearing up, but full on bawling. I'd realized at that moment that things are, in fact, starting to change. There are so many of you here, right now—artists, critics, academics—who stand for the things I stand for. It's like I was waiting for you all this time, and now you've arrived. Now we've arrived. Belonging is hard. But maybe it doesn't have to be.

Thank you.

2ND GENERATION IN TECH
Krys Freeman

Krys Freeman writes about authenticity at work, and about how leaning out doesn't mean you're giving up. I also love the reverence in this story for the grace and fortitude that we learn from our mothers and the women who came before us. Sometimes that strength is private, invisible to the world, and we are among the few who see it.

I was born in 1985, the year my mother graduated from Norman Thomas High School. Five years later she graduated from Baruch College with a B.S. in Computer Information Systems. She entered the workforce as a Programmer Analyst, her first stab at leveraging hard earned Pascal programming skills to achieve the kind of upward mobility not often associated with teenage moms. I was born eleven years before my mother would eventually take a role at Bloomberg. In taking this role, she would enter as, not only the first woman, but also the first black woman to join Bloomberg's "Console Room."

Her job was designing, implementing, and supporting all procedures on the Bloomberg Terminal. You could say "she made it." And as a function of her success, I've learned, from my mother, a similar way of working and ascending the ranks against the odds.

It's now 2015. If you meet my mother today, and read her CV, you won't hear about nor see the long list of hoops and hurdles she mastered to get to each new achievement. You won't get to peer back at those long college nights. You won't see her dozing, face planted in "C++ for you++" after putting me to bed. You certainly won't see her waking up to do it all over again.

You won't get to see her multiple expressions of shock during the first few days at Bloomberg when—despite the almost scientific process of her train ride, despite her naps on the train ending at the precise moment we were due to reach Grand Central station, despite her precise positioning of us at the right door in the right car of the 7 express (to get first crack at the exit pointed toward our transfer to the 6)—upon entering the doors of an office historically filled with male networking operators and engineers, she was asked "How the hell did you get here?"

The question of course, is much more invested in an answer explaining her professional merits than one explaining the actual feats it took to get this very young, very single mother to work on time. And, of course, no one will ever see how—from those first few days through the next nineteen years—she'd carry the weight of her work along with the weight of constant self-justification. She carried other goals and dreams too, deferred just a bit, in favor of creating opportunities for her children.

Nearly two decades later, you'll see that my mother has built a commendable career in managing Bloomberg's Development Operations Group. She made it.

She achieved this—as many women in male dominated fields do—by leading, advocating, and putting in long hours and hard work, every day diminishing the perceived differences between her and her peers. She did this no matter the cost or emotional toll. She did this, and still does it every day, with resolve, fortitude, and grace.

When I entered the business world as a technologist, I adopted some of those same characteristics. The complex mix of shaking off the stings and slights from colleagues (sometimes, based on my appearance alone) has often proved exhausting. Still, I learned from my mother that it's my job to show up every day doing no less than my best work.

Whether it was the inevitable awkward conversation about how people "love my hair," or the second glances when I entered a restroom (with my 5'10" athletic build and bow-tie) I was often reminded just how much I stuck out like a sore thumb. Still, I certainly got a better welcoming party than my mom. No one directly questioned my presence. However, their distance and the things they did say spoke volumes.

I spent a few years oscillating between inclinations to assimilate and just daring to be my authentic self. Both paths come with challenges.

In hindsight, it's easy to see how one might fall in line with Sheryl Sandberg's *Lean In* proposal. Sure, women should pursue our careers fearlessly and lead with self-confidence. Yes, every woman should take her seat at the table rather than lingering alongside in the margins. However, this seat comes at what cost? Does that seat require our silence or deference, in exchange for valida-tion of "culture fit?" And is it worth the cost to present an idea, only to have it dismissed at first, and then later validated when presented by someone else, be it a senior colleague, or a male one?

For many women, attempting leadership in their careers is a leap into murky territory, a territory not necessarily yielding Sandberg's promises. For women who do not fit in, leaning in does not always deliver automatic career success. Pressing on and leaning in, without giving real attention to oppositional circumstances, is part of pretending that there is no difference between us and our colleagues.

This minimization of difference is a lost opportunity to explore and value that difference. There is something valuable when someone like my mom (as opposed to a white man with a wife and permanent childcare) accom-plishes their educational and professional goals.

I don't fault anyone for choosing to engage, for taking their destiny into their own hands, however clumsy it might look at first, or how unnerving it may become over time.

But I do want to celebrate the daring few who disengage. I admire the few who choose to come to their own defense, to take a leap in the other direction. I commend those who lean out, choosing to value their own unique circumstances.

It took me more than a year to fully come to terms with the fact that in order to thrive, I needed to be myself. Part of this coming to terms meant working with and through my entrepreneurial desires. During my time as Director of Systems and Technology at GreenBiz, I had already begun taking on technology projects of my own. I began to offer freelance web development to friends and acquaintances starting their own business enterprises. I also started to take my passion project, HeLLa Rides, more seriously—iterating on the concept, rebranding it with a new name, and shopping it around to trusted friends and business contacts.

Working within small scrappy companies whet my appetite for running one of my own. As a startup employee, I had opportunities to test out my skills before diving in full-time. I once half-jokingly suggested to higher ups that what was missing from our events roster was a hackathon. We were running annual events assessing how technology advancements could catapult sustainability-oriented efficiencies; yet, we were missing key players in the conversation: developers.

That said, we were two weeks out from an event when I made the suggestion, so the idea wasn't going to fly. But not long after, my then-CEO tasked me with creating our first hackathon, slated as a complement for the next event on our calendar. The result? Hack City—a hackathon I produced (twice) with the help of a few digital assistant services and the labor of a few fantastic volunteers. In those two years, we were able to garner the support of Facebook, Salesforce, OnStar, SideCar, Code for America, the City of San Francisco and even the White House. The hackathon winners produced apps like Insite, a tool for facilities managers that could help provide actionable insight into building performance of their commercial portfolio, and Retrofitta (later renamed "Retrofunder") which was built to be a kickstarter for energy efficient retrofits. One of Retrofunder's members has since pivoted the idea into a company called RetroCap, a platform helping homeowners to complete an energy efficiency analysis, to assess the costs, and to connect them to service providers to complete the project.

Hack City strengthened personal relationships I had with business leaders whose focus on sustainability and technology matched my own, rather than making me mold myself to the ways and interests of others. It generated new relationships with Civic Tech enthusiasts who shared my interest for addressing the challenges affecting urban populations. It also offered new opportunities for me to share my skills.

Not long after the first event wrapped, I was invited to join the steering committee for another Hackathon in Boston (because of an experimental element I added to the Hack City hackathon that they wanted to repurpose). One of the winning apps in Boston, Crowd Comfort, has since evolved into a full-fledged startup company and has inked deals with the enterprise giant, General Electric. These were the hallmarks of achieving our main goal, raising the company's profile amongst the developer population local to the Bay Area.

It can be easy to overlook the growth that happens as we "lean in" to our work. It is even easier to overlook the resulting shrinkage that occurs as a process, the fatigue and trauma. However, the production of Hack City, though successful, taught me hard lessons about team building, delegation, and targeted marketing. Even with help, the time constraints, and (to be really transparent) the consistent creep of self-doubt, limited my ability to really cultivate the audience I was seeking at both events.

The people who did attend were great: creative thinkers, wildly idealistic and jazzed about hacking for prize money. Still, we wanted more attendance over all. But more than that, our efforts fell short of my personal goal: to better target and engage underserved communities of women of color, low income and tech-curious folks, who are sorely missing from tech spaces of all kinds. After realizing that this shortfall was as much an effect of my planning as it was the professional environment it was created in, I decided to make a change. I decided to leave my full-time job, using my personal difference as well as my difference of interest, to focus on creating options for underserved communities.

Leaning out, or walking away, doesn't mean that you've given up. This is especially true if that decision means a career that better suits your career ambitions or has a lower impact on your psyche. Hack City was my last official duty as an employee before going out on my own. I walked away from a full-time salary, benefits, and the comfort of a consistent paycheck in order to test the other possibilities. To see if I could, in fact, chart a path on my own.

I also walked away because I had lost my patience with the constant subtle (and not so subtle) interactions and comments with a bias against me, whether intended maliciously or done out of ignorance. I was unhappy, and I was fried, and did not have the language to address these kind of interactions in a way that wouldn't leave me further exasperated. I conceded that it was time to go.

Does this mean that I won't ever find myself in another corporate job or start-up environment, dealing with the same issues that I faced before? Certainly not. But I'm choosing me, valuing my unique interests, needs, and circumstances. I want to be able to authentically engage if I ever do, again, find myself in those environments.

Authenticity—valuing and acknowledging ourselves—can carry women a mighty long way. Authenticity is the place to begin before we ever find ourselves, in the interest of moving up, engaged in leaning in.

BEYOND THE BINARY: A/B TESTING TECH AND GENDER

Brook Shelley

I have gotten used to being a woman in tech. It's all that I've ever known, as I've been coding since 1997 and a woman for at least as long. Sometimes I wonder what it would be like to be a man. Brook Shelley knows. Brook Shelley is a woman but she used to be seen as a man. Her essay offers rare insights into gender and perception.

In 2002, I was a college student majoring in English. I began work in tech as a laptop help desk technician at my university. I wasn't excited about it per-se, but I did the math, and computer-based careers seemed significantly more lucrative than my options in English. At the beginning of my career, I was seen by the world, my hiring managers, and my coworkers as a man. But inside, I knew that I was really a woman. Ten years later, with my foot °firmly° in the door, I transitioned and was finally presenting as the woman that I'd been the entire time. Tech is a challenging field, but doubly so for those of us who are seen as women. My experiences both as someone seen as a man, and someone seen as a woman make for a strange A/B test on how perception of gender effects interactions, promotions, and comfort in the tech industry.

I'll be the first to admit that I had it somewhat easy. Even though I came from a lower-middle class family that struggled for food and rent at various times through-out my childhood, we had a computer for most of my life. My parents encouraged me to be involved on the Internet, and to learn how to solve technical challenges that ranged from, "How the hell do I get this game to launch," to "OK, it looks like we've got a virus." I quickly became the defacto IT staff for my family. My tech flu-ency outpaced even my father, who managed a defense tech company.

In so many ways, a young trans woman with access to the Internet is ideally set up for a future career in tech. In situations where I didn't feel like I could talk to any-one about my gender, or my questions about how to one day be able to come out, I could ask them online. This opportunity varies based on race, and access, but can help explain why many of us transgender folk end up in the tech field. Separated by a computer screen and a lot of wires, no one knows your gender; online, we are free to be seen for who we are.

So, by the time I made it to college, fixing computer issues was a cinch. I worked at the laptop help desk for my university, and built a network of (mostly men) who I would later have available when looking for new job options. I never felt like I fit in, but I was able to make a convincing enough show to not feel singled-out or isolated. As a camouflage, I learned their language, their mannerisms, and their attitudes. You may not be surprised to know that these were often misogynistic, homophobic, or transphobic. When so many things are under the auspice of a joke, and the environment is largely white or Asian men, the jokes tend toward the "I can't believe he said that," category. My friends enjoyed pushing the boundaries of what our group thought was acceptable. I admit that I enjoyed this too. I was fully complicit: in an effort to not be seen as a queer trans woman at any point, I would often be at the forefront of this horrible language. My thought was that if I was louder, and more gross than those around me, then I'd never worry about being on the other end of the punchline.

The fact that we often didn't target anyone specific, and made these jokes amongst ourselves, does not remove the damage that they caused. We were perpetuating (through humor) a culture of oppression. Growing up in a conservative, Christian household, sexist, racist and homophobic views were encouraged from childhood. I was taught that women were obviously less capable than men, and would be better at home. Homosexuality was a sin, and a choice. Other religions, and other racial or ethnic groups, were not the same as us, and would need our help. Missionary work was encouraged. I was held up as a good example when I challenged others on their views around these topics. I was touted for "defending my faith" by harassing, picking verbal fights with, and debating less bigoted students. Throughout all of this, I knew that if my family were aware of my gender and sexuality, I would potentially be houseless, disowned, and on the street. This was further emphasized by my father when I was a teenager. At some point that I don't fully remember, I must have indicated my desire to transition. What I do remember, vividly, is his reaction: "If you ever transition or become a woman, I will disown you." At twelve-years-old, this was an impossible fight for me. So, despite appearing to the world as a guy, I dressed-up as myself in private, and learned more about feminism and queer sexualities.

In the workplace, this dichotomy . . . this split-life . . . continued to haunt me. Even in situations where I knew that I was enacting or overhearing misogyny or homophobia, I knew that to respond would mean exclusion and a new set of "jokes" targeting me. So I participated. I listened. I tried to do what I could to get ahead, all the while knowing that I would not be as able to succeed if I was really honest. In any workplace, you quickly learn the power structures, and for most workplaces, those are male power structures. I learned that to fit in would be to continue my illusion of masculinity. I would drink Scotch, laugh raucously, and boast of my prowess like the rest of my coworkers, all the while cringing inside. It hurt to lie to myself and others, but it paid the bills. When I saw or heard women being objectified, mocked, or questioned, I didn't want to be singled-out. Sometimes it was a lack of courage, and other times, I just knew that someone would find out my secret.

Being trans was a weight of concealment. My math went like this: if you know I am trans, you will think I am a monster. I will lose my job, and be disowned from my friends, and my career. My family will not want me around, and I will fall apart. In the way that many structures are built over years, my complex reasoning for playing along silently grew around me.

But, it was also a house of cards. When I finally came out, I found that the systems I'd built did not crumble in the ways I worried about. If anything, I continued to be my own worst enemy. No one openly questioned my work at my first job, but I felt questioned anyway. As I interviewed, I was on a razor's edge, wondering when someone would denounce me as a fake. When this didn't happen, I was able to see the terror of being seen as a woman. The patronizing looks. The surprise at my performance, skill, or knowledge. The desire, even internally, to embody ignorance about certain topics. The strategies I'd always known, about how to disappear in a room when I needed to, how to not upset the delicate male ego by being too forthright. I still do these things some days. It doesn't feel good, but it is useful. These are strategies that all of us, all women can use as a second nature. These are the survival tools of modern patriarchy. Suddenly my gender—my femaleness—was as relevant as my performance. Am I being praised because I am a woman, and they have a low bar for my performance? Am I being judged harshly for that outburst because I am seen as shrill, hormonal, or emotionally unbalanced? Why do I suddenly need to justify every technical suggestion? It was strange how quickly my prowess, or at least other's perception of my prowess, disappeared.

The more I consider these aspects of misogyny in tech, the more I realize I felt them before my transition too. Sometimes the things I chalked up to my personality or skills were likely the men in the room scenting my reluctance. My imposter syndrome. My woman-under-patriarchy fear of taking up too much space. I had a few mentors over the years, and their advice to me always felt wrong. When I tried to put it into motion, I experienced radically different outcomes from what they prepared me for.

An example:

I was always told to under promise, and over deliver. This is a typical IT trope—the idea being that if you tell someone it'll take you a month longer to implement than it actually does, you will look even better when you're able to finish early, and under-budget. I saw men around me use this tool successfully many times. Their contributions were praised, and their prowess was sought when making strategic decisions. However, even before transition, my proposals were met with disdain, questions, or disbelief. Surely I had misspoken. "That can't take 2 months," or "I think you just need to try harder."

It's very difficult to help a company with technical things when the people you work with doubt your ability to accomplish those tasks. This was made all the more painful by the fact that often, their ignorance was the catalyst for their doubt. "They hired me because I know about these things, so why can't they just trust me to actually deliver?" I'd think. But their doubt and mistrust was often because of my feminine markers.

A lot of the advice I'd heard didn't seem to apply to women at all. Speaking up, advocating for yourself at meetings, bringing new ideas. These all led to myself or those around me being seen as bossy or bitchy. These ideas would be dismissed—I would be told "that's nice"—but the same idea would be received with much admiration when later suggested by a guy. Men would flirt with me, but when I'd brush them off, they'd begin to dismiss me. I quickly learned how to express "I'm not interested because I'm gay, but I'll play along a little and make you feel like your attention is wanted" just to get through the day. As a woman in tech, you have to navigate so much gender politics. It's a constant and painful additional aspect of showing up to work and getting the job done.

The workplace was often disturbing in its abuse of women. Women aren't always aware of what men say behind closed-doors, but before transition I heard quite a lot more than I'd wanted. "Check out her ass," or "Whoa, nice boobs," followed by a whistle. These happened more times that I can count, in my presence. There would be arguments over who got to help the girl or girls the team deemed "hot." Married men, single men, young, or old—they all treated the office as a dating pool; a Tinder where their power would obviously entice a nubile girl into their arms. It was bizarre. When behavior was brought up to other men in power, it was often laughed-off. "Oh, you know Jim . . . he's just like that. He's harmless."

But it wasn't harmless. It hurt. It hurt women whose careers depended on being taken seriously; on not just how attractive she was, but how she could perform her job. It hurt women who would have accusations and whispers of "who'd she blow?" in hushed-tones if she °did° succeed. Of course everyone knew that °she° was sleeping with him. That's the only way she got where she was. For women who managed teams, this was all the more destructive of their ability to effectively lead a group of coworkers. And when any woman actually °did° engage in a relationship with her coworker, or sleep with someone in the tech scene, she was immediately a pariah. Even my fellow women would turn on her in an instant. "Yeah, she's a slut."

Men could cheat or sleep around with very little comment. Coworkers and upper-management who were either divorced or separated due to infidelity outnumbered the ones who were monogamously partnered. Most of my coworkers and friends in the industry would usually have a story about "how horrible his wife was," or how he was "kind of a dog, but he's effective." Some bosses who were somewhat attractive would garner a James Bond-like glow. Their philandering yielded them adoring fans.

The double-standard was so visible to me, because I could also see the two-facedness that men presented behind their closed-doors, and then at large. My teammates would occasionally discuss "what a whore" one person was, while laughing about the sexual conquests of another male coworker. Getting wasted and showing up to work hungover was met with applause and winks. One coworker even showed up with a black eye and nearly broken nose from his drunken exploits the night before. Women, I'd noticed, were always expected to be chipper, well-dressed, and attentive.

The well-dressed part baffles me. I'd seen the ways in which men could succeed in hoodies and flip-flops. In some circles, that was the secret handshake that said "I'm one of the dudes, I'm trustworthy and smart." For us, there isn't an accepted dress-code that creates that trust. If we do not want to emulate men with hoodies and jeans, we are expected to either wear the clothing of the young, sexy office girlfriend, or the well-to-do mom. Neither of these uniforms creates inclusion in the tech circle. And often these clothes are pointed to by the harasser as an excuse for bad behavior. I knew that I, as a woman, can wear whatever I want—that I neither need, nor want male approval—but it was frustrating that as soon as I showed up to work in a dress, I got either stares of lust, or questions about showing "so much leg." I had one manager who even attempted to pull my skirt down, and would warn me to sit differently, often. Despite being trans, I had also absorbed the messages culture teaches our young girls about being prim, proper, and chaste in our dress; I just didn't care for them.

In the offices where we had a kitchen, it was usually me, or one of the other girls who'd offer to take dishes into the kitchen, or wash them. It was women who would set up for company events. Women who silently took care of all the small things around parties, and office launches. These activities were met with the occasional flowers or "thank yous," but rarely with promotions, raises, or recognition. It was very clear that it was expected of us. In offices full of boys, someone has to be the mother. It is horrible to be the office mother.

At work, I often have to justify my ideas more now. Once I could, to some degree, answer technical questions with "oh, that sounds like it would work," but now I had to pile on reasons and justifications. As many women in tech observe, I too saw men presenting the same or very similar ideas with quick acceptance, while I could tell my questioner was clearly in doubt about my skill set. Each new company is another place to need to prove oneself, as well as each new tech event. From what I can tell, it is possible to build a cachet to some degree with the company we stay with, but if we move around, women have the same conversations to justify their intelligence and knowledge ad nauseum.

Outside of work too, I would run into expectations I hadn't before being seen as a woman. Eyebrows would raise when I mentioned what field I worked in, and raise even higher when they found out I was in a technical position. I'd find myself feeling like I needed to justify my work experience to friends and acquaintances. Suddenly I was wondering if being seen as an engineer was also to be seen as more masculine. Obviously this is ridiculous, as many of the modern inventions and discoveries we rely on came from women of this and previous generations, but the stereotype of the male engineer and start-up worker plagued me.

The one way I have found to soothe a number of these issues, or at least commiserate, is to surround myself with other women in tech, both at my own company, and by going to women's tech events. I've found plenty of women who understand intersectional feminism, who are smart, and funny, and who share with me stories of abuse, harassment, and fear. We also build each other up, encourage, and teach. We support each other during the ups and downs of the industry and life. Strong networks of fellow tech feminists make working in tech possible for me, and many other women. If we were truly only ever in a boys club, I don't know many women would still be in our industry.

When I consider the differences in experience, I wonder what my life would look like if I'd transitioned at twelve, when I first had the courage to bring up my womanhood. I fear it would be significantly worse. The early 2000s were not kind to trans women, and considering I would likely have been kicked out of my house, I likely wouldn't have made it to college, or even into IT. But, the one thing I come back to, is that then, I would probably have less complicated feelings about both misogyny, and my internalization of it. However, this complexity gives me a unique window into the places in tech that are specifically toxic to women, and a strong sense that we women must be involved and active in making a difference for each other.

LET'S TALK ABOUT SEX . . . UAL DISCRIMINATION

Gesche Haas

Sexual harassment and gender discrimination are all too common, but many women fear taking action. When a VC in Berlin emailed Gesche Haas: "Hey G. I am not leave [sic.] Berlin without having sex with you. Deal?" Gesche stood up for herself. She writes here about going public with that experience.

There is no denying that in many ways men "run this world." I may be a woman but I have always believed that anything is possible if you set your mind to it . . . and work your ass off.

I spent many years working on my companies before becoming Internet-famous for being sexually harassed by a VC in Germany. As soon as I came out with my story, I was flooded with letters from other women who had been similarly treated. They've asked me . . . what made me brave enough to speak up? And how did I feel?

Let's be honest, it took what felt like forever for me to sort out my feelings about the situation.

On one hand, I was proud of my refusal to accept the said behavior—regardless of the potential risks. However, one can only imagine what a huge time-suck in mental distraction and self-questioning this incident provoked. Imagine how painful this felt to an entrepreneur who carefully and meticulously optimizes every second of her life. It drained me. Early on, the email led to many sleepless nights during which I felt conflicted, unable to stop analyzing the situation. Should I do something or nothing at all? Countless hours were spent drafting anonymous blog posts about what had happened. Embarking on this journey, I never expected the story to eventually make its way into the press—but when it did, it went viral. The aftermath was so consuming that my productivity and focus was immensely impacted for several weeks.

In addition to the (unwelcome) distraction from work, I am also the first to admit that becoming a figure in the media's discourse regarding sexual discrimination had never been part of my five-year plan. Yet, if you Google my name today there is no doubt left that it is now my "claim to fame." Case in point, you are reading a piece right now about sexism, written by me.

Adding to the outer world's perception of my situation were also many inner conflicts. I pride myself on being a very easy-going person who has no problem "hanging with the boys." I also strongly believe people ought to be able to do what they want to do without being judged. So, was I in the wrong for calling this man out? Could I not just pretend it never happened and go on with my life without all these distractions?

I tried. I couldn't.

What was the harm caused? In my particular case, I can tell you what it felt like receiving a very sexually charged email after a business interaction. It screamed: "I think you have little to no worth to me in a business context—you only have value to me merely by owning a vagina—and there is nothing you can, or will, do about me deciding to openly communicate this to you."

To a large extent it came down to feeling powerless . . .

Yet, I cannot emphasize enough that the feeling of "having control" and being able to act accordingly is about so much more than the gender ratio. There are multiple studies that indicate that we need to feel like we are in control in order to feel happy.[1] The VC fund First Round Capital has published a blog post stating quite clearly that we need be happy in order to be effective founders.[2]

---

[1] https://medium.com/thelist/hacking-happiness-90fde 4d931bd

[2] http://firstround.com/review/Heres-Why-Founders-Should-Care-about-Happiness/

How can we be effective founders if we don't even feel we have the power to demand from others (whatever their gender) to treat us with respect?

For this and so many other reasons I know that speaking up was the only right thing to do. I initially felt conflicted around my identity as a "sexism fighter" because it implies that a woman feels victimized. But that no longer is my belief. In fact, I think the exact opposite is the case.

I now (with pride) say that sexism is something I will not tolerate.

The publicizing of the story felt like I ripped the lid off Pandora's box. I received thousands of messages by women who had gone through similar stories and felt incredibly empowered by seeing someone speak up about it publicly. It was eye-opening seeing that I was clearly not alone with all those inner conflicts and how my actions helped other women. There were just as many men who reached out with incredibly touching notes expressing support for my decision, many voicing how appalled they were and some went so far as to profusely thank me for creating a better environment for their daughters to grow up in.

Of course there was also negative backlash—and it did sting. But this was also one of the biggest life learning lessons I have ever received—about being able to believe in yourself and not allowing anything or anyone to stop you from doing what you know is the right thing.

Yes, I've realized first hand that finding solutions won't be smooth sailing. But on my journey I've also learned that no matter how tricky the situation is we cannot not shy away from these difficult fights.

I believe that as women in tech we have a heightened responsibility. As entrepreneurs we are highly skilled problem-solvers; it's what we do. We are change-makers, used to raising eyebrows. Yet if we want the opportunity to question the status quo in a business context we must also be ready to do the same for ourselves on a deeply personal level.

Having had the realizations and breakthroughs I've had, I would not think twice about embarking on it again, despite how much it may have disrupted my workflow. These are things most men do not have to go through but I do believe that with every time a woman decides to stand up, fewer of our sex will have to deal with it again.

There will always be some men (and women) who, similar to my grandfather, will need tangible evidence in order to see "women's value." Rather than feel intimidated by this, let's accept the challenge. Let's command respect. Yes, what all of this really comes down to is respecting ourselves. As Eleanor Roosevelt said: "No one can make you feel inferior without your own consent."

Honestly, I have no clue if the man who sent me that email now respects me more. But what I do know is that I can look in the mirror and respect myself knowing I did not just accept such behavior. By commanding worth and demonstrating that I have control over my destiny—I can now finally return to giving my entrepreneurial dreams the shot they deserve.

ON BEING A FEMALE IN VENTURE CAPITAL

Erica Swallow

Erica Swallow first wrote "On Being a Female in Venture Capital" after a summer internship at General Catalyst, while studying at the MIT Sloan School of Business. It is no secret that Venture Capital is a male-dominated field, but few women are willing to go on the record to discuss the details. Senior women in VC (or women wishing to become senior in VC) cannot risk rocking the boat. That makes Swallow's story all the more important.

Her original essay "On Being A Female in Venture Capital" is reprinted here, along with a new essay offering us a more in-depth, personal account of women and venture capital.

Standing in my cubicle, I heard a deep, muffled voice in the office kitchen exclaim, "We should hire some more girls here!" On the other side of that conversation, another twenty-something male responded, "We have Erica, the summer intern." And that was that. The two went on as if the problem had been solved with the existence of one female, associate-level, summer-only intern.

Throughout my summer internship as an associate at Boston-based venture capital firm General Catalyst, I was consistently reminded of my place as a woman in a man's world. Don't get me wrong, I thoroughly enjoyed my internship, as it was an opportunity to learn about an industry I previously had no experience in, and I respect and admire the colleagues I worked alongside.

The fact of the matter, though, is that women— beyond the high-heel-studded secretaries and assistants—don't exist in venture capital, and that makes for a strange environment when you're the only woman working on an investment team. A paltry 4.2 percent of partner-level decision-makers in venture capital are women, even trailing behind the stat that only 4.6 percent of Fortune 500 CEOs are women.

In my case at GC, there were no other women in sight on the investing side. Sure, women existed on the human resources, marketing, and support staff teams— but what message do you think I heard when I was the only woman, at a lowly intern position, sitting in on founder pitches and investment meetings? In short: VC is no place for a woman.

The only time being a woman had any cachet was recruitment for the firm's co-ed softball team, which was part of a league that mandated teams maintain a minimum female membership. I heard our team discussing one woman's participation on a particular night, "You don't have to come tonight, if you don't want. We don't really need you, since we already have enough women." So, the only thing that made her valuable on the team was her gender? I'm sure that was comforting for her and every other woman in ear-shot. I, for one, was disturbed.

It's no wonder, then, that my proposal to research "female founders" as a sourcing opportunity for the summer was turned down. When I suggested the topic, pointing to the fact that it would be great to have more women in the tech startup ecosystem, and that I had found data that proved there was a bias toward men in VC, my project lead said it was a great topic, but something that couldn't exist without me, a woman, coming on full-time. That is to say, all the sourcing I would do over the summer, focused on female founders, wouldn't be a project the firm was interested in continuing after I was gone—because, hey, who wants to focus on sourcing females only? That should be a woman's job, right?

Now, let me just pause and say how much my summer mentor—a person I consider a friend and admire to the max—cared about setting me up for success. His aim for my internship was for me to have a wonderful time, utilize some of my strengths to add value for the firm, and come away with a deliverable that lasted long after I was gone. Therefore, he pointed me in a direction that would be most useful for the firm after I left. It just so happens, though, that mapping out the world of female founders was deemed not-so-useful. That wasn't his fault—it was just a truth we accepted. We then moved on to other topics, and I finally chose to research "the future of work," another topic I was passionate about pursuing given my own experiences as a non-traditional worker.

My interest in researching and sourcing female founders for deals, though, rose from a Harvard/Wharton/MIT study that found venture capitalists prefer startup pitches from attractive men, above women—and equally disturbing—above unattractive men. In a three-part study, researchers studied gender and physical attractiveness by having investors choose startup pitches to "fund" from a real competition, voice recordings, and video recordings. "Across all three experiments, investors strongly preferred men over women," US News reported. "In fact, men were more likely to win funding by as much as 60 to 70 percent. Attractive men were viewed even more favorably, getting an additional 36 percent jump in 'pitch success.'"

These findings, to me, are just plain disheartening. But to an investor, I thought, this might say "opportunity," given market biases. Nope. Wasn't the case. I think it said something like, "Not specialized enough, not important to focus on, and not where the money's at."

Female participation in startup entrepreneurship is dismal. Women have won just 7 percent of venture capital funding and founded just 11 percent of America's high growth ventures. There are many factors that lead to these low numbers, but it's disappointing that part of the problem stems from who's making decisions in VC. When men prefer "attractive men" and find their pitches more "persuasive, logical and fact-based than were the same pitches narrated by a female voice," there's obvious bias at play.

My summer in venture capital, while educational and eye-opening, showed me—among other things—that entrepreneurship is even harder than I imagined. A former colleague of mine called me up last week to discuss her new role in venture capital—she joined a small firm in Silicon Valley after three years at Google, starting out as a community manager and being promoted to a program manager position. We spoke on a number of topics, but one she asked me about, seemingly embarrassed for bringing up, was about "getting hit on." She had heard from a male colleague that she should "clarify what every meeting is about," or else she might get herself tangled in a situation with an investor or founder more interested in her than her work. I was shocked to hear that anecdote, but I shared with her my own experiences, of overhearing bro convos and feeling a bit left out of the culture, since I was, by my own existence as a woman, different from everyone else.

I'll look back at my internship and remember the beautiful report my team and I put together on the future of work, the "product testing" I did to receive Uber ice cream and free Postmates cannolis from Mike's Pastry, the flowers my boyfriend delivered as a "secret admirer" one day, and the firm's summer party my favorite colleagues and I put together. I'll chuckle at the memory of building my own standing desk out of printing paper reams. And I'll always have my "Camp Catalyst" sweatshirt and "General Alley Catalysts" bowling tee to remind me of the outings the company sponsored. Reading Brad Feld's "Venture Deals" (a Sloan alum, I might add!) in two sittings, because it's that good will stick in my memory, and Monday morning investment team meetings have their special place in my heart.

My summer internship was full of many wonderful memories. I won't forget, though, the burning sensation I felt in my face every time a secretary walked into a room to remind a partner his next meeting had arrived. Or the strange pride I felt when the only woman on our bowling team hit a strike, putting her ahead of some of our male colleagues—even though we were on the same team, mind you! It will take years for the feeling of outsider-ness to fade. And I count this experience as one more step toward educating myself, a part of the millennial generation, that a lot needs to change in our time at the helm.

While I'm not sure what the future holds for me, I'm drawn toward making sure women are better represented at the table in the worlds of entrepreneurship and venture capital. How to make that happen, I'm not sure. But I'm open to ideas.

VENTURE CAPITAL AND THE CASE OF THE WHINY WOMAN

Erica Swallow

I never thought I'd become one of those "whiny women" who make a public ruckus about the crap cards dealt to women in the workplace. But after a summer internship in venture capital—an industry plagued by a small and declining number of women decision-makers—I had become that very same stereotype.

Growing up in a family that lived below the poverty line, I had always experienced inequalities. But I was taught that you reap what you sow. It had always been my understanding that my family had found itself at the bottom of society because my single mother hadn't gone to college, and the deadbeat father figures in my life had not only failed to secure a proper education, but also had varying degrees of drug and alcohol addictions. Statistics, I reasoned, were not on my side. I was the product of a multi-divorce, poor, single-parent household, growing up in the South, a place of constricting opportunities. It was my family's fault, I had told myself. I imagined that if we had built things differently, we would have been our town's doctors and lawyers.

It was this childhood belief in meritocracy that led me to believe that women who whined about their workplaces were just poorly suited for their environments. They, or their mentors hadn't set themselves up for success, I believed. It was on the woman, then, to get over her environment and make something better of herself. "If you can't stand the heat, get out of the kitchen," the old adage, so ironically, goes.

And so, it wasn't until I had experienced my own gender-related professional travesty that I realized these whistleblowers of ages past had legitimacy. I wouldn't posit that every woman who's ever thrown down the gender card is in the right, but after a summer in venture capital [VC], I realized that some industries are completely unwelcoming to women, and should be seriously reformed.

I remember the moment my acceptance letter for New York University came in the mail. I had been checking the mailbox for days, and on that fateful morning, I opened our weathered, tin mailbox to find a large, white, thick envelope. I didn't have to open it to know the tides were changing for me—every college applicant knows that big envelopes mean good things. Finally, all those seeds I had sown were coming to harvest, and I saw a horizon of change before me.

Four years as an undergraduate student in New York City and four more years of work experience flew by, and I came out of that Big Apple journey a new person. I had come from little Arkansas with only small-town, all-American experiences to speak of, but my time in New York redefined what was possible for a country girl: I had accumulated more than a couple dozen international trips, had landed coveted positions at respected organizations including *The New York Times* and Saatchi & Saatchi, and had been invited to speak at world-recognized conferences, such as SXSW, WOMMA Summit, and Social Media Brasil. I finally had some of the accolades necessary to be a "somebody."

In 2013, I enrolled as an MBA candidate at the MIT Sloan School of Business, yet another example of my drive to be the best I could be. I had been the first to graduate from college in my family, and that year I became the first to attend grad school. It was then that I became interested in venture capital. Prior to business school, I had spent a few years as a technology journalist, writing about startups for Mashable, *Forbes*, and other notable publications. I had also founded my own consulting firm, planning and executing social media and digital marketing strategy work for startups and small businesses. I grew to love the startup ethos and work culture. I started another business, this time a tech startup, and entered b-school with five months of foundership under my belt.

I was working on a peer-to-peer delivery startup, called Deliverish. At the time, I believed business school would give me time to determine if this new venture was the right direction for me. Little did I realize, juggling business school—especially first year—and a business is potentially the worst idea I had ever thought up.

My team and I disbanded in December 2013, at the end of the first semester. It turns out having teammates in three states is also a really bad idea; but we were lucky to have had the time that b-school allowed to test out ideas. In the end, we determined margins were too low and the competition—including Amazon, eBay, Google, WunWun, Uber, and Postmates—would eat us alive. To this day, I'm pretty sure the delivery industry is going to be a brutal death match, and it's better to be an observer than a participant. So, I'll just sit happily on the sidelines as the incumbents kill each other in a pricing war.

Even though I knew it was the right decision, closing up shop on Deliverish was one of the hardest decisions I've ever made. I'm glad my teammates and I knew when to stop, because continuing would have been hell. After Deliverish, I was completely drained of inspiration. I went through a few months of wandering, trying to figure out my life's purpose. That's when I latched onto venture capital.

At the time, I was working with a team of young leaders from across Boston on a student partnership called Rough Draft Ventures. Funded by Boston-based venture capital firm General Catalyst, Rough Draft Ventures is a venture capital-like fund run by students for students. All of the partners are current students from across Boston universities, including Harvard, Tufts, MIT, Olin, and Boston University, who meet weekly to see student entrepreneurs pitch their startups for real funding. Rough Draft invests up to $25,000 in those startups, which are run by world-class founders building world-changing technologies.

Rough Draft was my first taste of venture. I had found my way to the group through one of its founders, Peter Boyce II, who I had known from the New York tech scene. I considered him to be one of the coolest and most interesting people I had ever met. He was one of the first people I reached out to after moving to Boston—I wanted his advice on how to best get to know the Boston technology community. I knew he'd know exactly what I should do to get the most out of my time in Boston.

I told Peter I had an interest in understanding venture capital as a startup founder. I had imagined myself dropping out of school after my first year, and needing to raise capital for Deliverish. Peter had listened to my options and ideas, and he threw another out there: Rough Draft Ventures, the opportunity to meet fellow students from across Boston, see pitches from the most innovative startups in the community, and learn about venture capital by doing it. That was exactly what I was looking for. Peter invited me to join the team, an opportunity I couldn't refuse, and I started off my school year by joining this group of highly inspiring, technology-loving people. I had found a home.

For my entire first year at business school, I prioritized Rough Draft over my other commitments. Every Monday, we met for three to four hours for the pitch meetings; I had tons of coffee meetings with founders; and I focused some of my efforts on developing a monthly student entrepreneurs' Meetup, given my past experience with community management. Rough Draft ran like a beautiful machine, where everyone contributed their strengths and worked on their weaknesses, bringing in great teams from their various networks and communities, and working together to get more students excited about building companies.

From Arkansas to New York to Boston, I had gone from scraping by and occasionally living without electricity and water to helping fund projects that would change our community, lives, and economy. I realized that a role in venture capital could potentially be the most impactful next step for me.

The Big Opportunity

Every weekend, I found myself looking forward to the Rough Draft Ventures partner meetings, which took place on Monday evenings. I loved hearing about new technologies and seeing how teams were solving some of the biggest issues they had encountered in their own lives. Seeing a founder bubble with excitement at his own work is one of the most contagious feelings I've experienced. You can't help but want to help out people who are working on things that matter and that they are dead set on fixing.

At the end of my first year in b-school, I found myself pondering my summer internship opportunities. I had begun working on another startup project, a technology that turns your smartphone into a thermometer, without the use of hardware. But my teammates and I had decided it wasn't what we wanted to spend our time on over the summer.

I thought back over my first year, considering the activities that had most excited me, quickly realizing that I lived and breathed for my Rough Draft experiences. More than that, it was the people I was working with that I loved—the partnership was truly the most inspiring group of people I had spent time with since moving to Boston. My path was clear: I reached out to the Rough Draft co-founders, Peter and Nitesh—both General Catalyst full-timers—to see if they would be interested in working with me over the summer. We all loved each other, so it was a clear fit, personally. We talked it out, and Nitesh brought me on as a summer associate, working on the early-stage investment team with a focus on sourcing startups relevant to the future of work.

Prior to business school, I hadn't imagined that I'd be spending my summer in venture. My mentors had told me it'd be wise, but I had always seen myself starting my own company. After year one and my time as a Rough Drafter, I knew that it was a viable option. I loved working with entrepreneurs and digging into new ideas, and I couldn't imagine having a job that actually paid me to do so.

I spent the week before my internship reading books on the industry and scoping out my interest areas, the firm's structure, and potential side projects. I was ready to make a splash at the firm; little did I know, it was going to be a splash that no one—not even I—expected.

Venture Capital: No Place For a Woman

The date is Monday, August 4, 2014. My internship had ended the previous Friday, and I was preparing to give my mentors a final project update. I had identified 350 potential target investments, conducted 66 founder meetings, interviewed 17 experts on the future of work, and culled my findings into a 106-slide Keynote presentation, complete with nine trends shaping the way we work and three investments I found particularly intriguing.

Two hours before my final meeting, *The Wall Street Journal* ran a profile of my summer experience as a woman in venture capital, titled "Female Intern Finds Venture Capital 'No Place For A Woman.'" Writer Deborah Gage had got wind of my story and reached out to conduct an interview. The entire venture capital industry, it seemed, was up in arms about a blog post I had penned for the MIT Sloan blog a week prior about the key issue I experienced working in venture that summer: being a woman.

Indeed, that entire week since publishing the post was an utter shitshow. I felt that I was voicing an opinion that was important to share, but the firm felt I was attacking them, as did many of the *Wall Street Journal* commenters, who stated that as industry insiders, they felt I was immature and incompetent for speaking out. They called me an "entitled prima donna," a "petulant child," a "social Marxist," and a "misguided social justice warrior" for sharing my story.

In the post [reprinted in *Lean Out* as "On Being a Female in Venture Capital"], I outlined both the pros and cons of my summer internship, with a focus on the unconscious bias I witnessed every day in the office. Being the only woman in all of the meetings General Catalyst set for me was pretty sad. And being the only woman on the early-stage investment team was also a weird social dynamic. I was disheartened to see that the majority of the women that graced the firm's halls were in administrative positions. On a daily basis, they worried about loading the dishwasher, ushering guests in, and ordering lunch while all of the men did the heavy lifting investments that brought home the bacon.

I had spent my entire adult life as a gender minority. I went to undergraduate business school and had chosen to ante up again with graduate business school—business schools tend to have an average female enrollment of around 30 percent. I had also worked in the technology, media, and advertising sectors, all industries dominated by men.

Venture capital, as it turned out, though, is the worst offender I've ever been a part of. The industry is made up of just 6 percent of women partners, down from 10 percent in 1999, according to the 2014 Diana Project report entitled "Women Entrepreneurs 2014: Bridging the Gender Gap in Venture Capital." Not only are women underrepresented in one of the most important economy-defining industries in the nation, but they are also dropping out of the industry, as that report makes clear.

This impacts funding for women. Venture firms with female partners are more than twice as likely to invest in startups with a woman on the executive team and more than three times as likely to invest in a company with a female CEO, the Diana Project report states. So the lack of women representation in venture firms leads to significantly less funding for female entrepreneurs.

This would—perhaps—be understandable if women entrepreneurs sucked at doing business. But study after study shows that women perform just as well, if not better, than men in business settings. Businesses with a woman on the executive team, the Diana Project found, are more likely to have higher valuations at both first and last funding (64 percent higher and 49 percent higher, respectively).

In stating that venture capital was "no place for a woman" in my original post, I had hoped to get the attention of the industry and explain just how ostracized I felt, based solely on my gender.

As I learned, my experience wasn't unique. In fact, many female investors reached out to thank me for sharing my honest take on being a woman in venture, because it had been their experience as well, but they were too afraid to speak up, knowing that the consequences would be career-ruining.

I, to my discredit, didn't exactly realize the predicament I was getting myself into by blogging about my internship. First of all, I didn't realize how the huge gender imbalance would affect me. I was used to being a minority, and it hadn't been a problem to date. I didn't see how a little bit of bro culture would affect me now.

Furthermore, it wasn't until after a year at Rough Draft, when I was interning in venture "for real," that I realized our student partnership had been 50 percent female and had a diverse representation of racial, ethnic, and international opinions on the team. My exposure to "venture capital" had been via a sort of utopian view of what VC could be, but it had only been a sliver of what it's really like to work in venture capital. I had, then, miscalculated what it would be like to work with the General Catalyst team, based on my interactions with their student partnership project, Rough Draft Ventures. Had I spent more time in the office during working hours and met with more teammates prior to inquiring about an internship, I might have realized a cultural misfit. Lastly, I had overlooked the cultural taboo I was breaking in venture about speaking up about an internal issue. Granted, I had been asked by the MIT Sloan blog editor to write a post on being a woman in venture for Women's Week. I cut myself a little slack there, but I can see how industry commentators might see me as dimwitted for taking action in the way I did.

No one wants to be tagged as the nagging female who won't shut up about gender inequality. I learned through experience that the feedback and backlash that comes from sharing the raw, but commonly shared experience, of being a woman in venture capital is not for the faint of heart. The trolls come out in masses, wielding their best put-downs.

This can't, though, be the future of VC. For the sake of everyone involved, we must work together to build an inclusive culture within this community, a community that adds so much value to the U.S. and world economies.

Solving Gender Inequality Once and For All

Coming out alive and well on the other end of the backlash I received for voicing my concerns about the VC gender gap, I've been on a mission to understand what investors think about their industry's gender imbalance and to extract lessons from their experiences. Hundreds of coffee meetings, phone calls, and emails later, I'm heartened to know that there are many good people in the venture community who are working actively to speak out in favor of closing the gender gap.

From the National Venture Capital Association (NVCA), to the women-led firms that are popping up, to the partners who want to see more diverse people—and thus opinions—at their firms, there are many great souls ready to take this issue head-on.

While I haven't found the silver bullet that will level the playing field for women overnight, the partners I've been in discussions with have pointed me to three key takeaways that will influence the way the industry goes about solving the gender gap:

- Decisions must come from within. So far, the conversation on how to solve the gender imbalance in VC has come from outsiders, such as myself, who have dipped their toes in and are appalled by the discrimination that happens inside venture. I only spent a summer in venture so far; what do I know? Change, unfortunately, can only be made when the insiders believe it needs to happen. Furthermore, it is the insiders who are on the ground day-to-day who will be able to brainstorm solutions that actually make sense, fit within budgets, and bring about real gains.

- Men are a critical part of the solution. People look at gender imbalance as a woman's problem. It is, however, everyone's problem. When we limit the pool of potential investments by gender, due to our own structural shortcomings, we're cutting out a lot of opportunity. Firms that realize women and other minorities are ripe for investment, and that they are currently being devalued in the marketplace, will ultimately perform better. It's called portfolio diversification for a reason. Men, who represent more than 90 percent of the industry's decision-making power, need to lead this conversation. The time where it was acceptable to have an all-women's committee working on the "women problem" is over. Now is the time for 50/50 partnership in solving this people problem.

- An industry coalition must exist to share best practices. Venture capitalists want direction on this topic, but have little time to think about how their firms could improve practices. If a group of progressive industry insiders made time to work together and disseminate best practices, the impact could be huge. Hiring and cultural awareness, for example, are afterthoughts for VCs, and when hiring does come into play, it's often a "pattern-seeking" sort of activity: "I went to Yale and was in the DKE fraternity, as were my partners and favorite colleagues. So, I'm going to recruit there!" An industry-level task force could set best practices for hiring and building inclusive cultures, so that VCs could easily digest and act upon these learnings.

While I have one year left at business school, I'm still interested in helping build a group of individuals within the venture capital community who care about researching and solving the gender gap issue in this industry. Although I don't yet have the perfect solutions to solve the problem, I do know that a group of dedicated advocates is a must-have to get started. Currently the VC gender topic is relegated to one-off panels, conferences, and media blips without much sustainable dialogue and effort toward change.

Such a group could work on creating case studies of firms that are working to hire more talented women, focusing on how to: build a hiring funnel, shape a firm culture so that women and other diverse candidates feel welcome, and address gender issues that arise internally. This group could build a central database for these case studies, resources, best practices, academic research, and media regarding the VC gender gap. It could also offer consulting and training services to firms that are facing issues in resolving internal gender bias issues. The group could even standardize an industry report for making diversity metrics more transparent across firms, creating an incentive for firms to hire with more diversity in mind. The possibilities are endless, as long as a dedicated organization is set up to own the issue and its solutions.

I'm confident, given the time I've spent interviewing influential insiders, that there are plenty of advocates ready to take a stand. Now, it's just a matter of building a platform on which they can be hoisted to call their colleagues to action.

This, my friends, is the beginning of the next chapter of my life.

BUT WHAT IF IT'S KILLING YOU?

anna anthropy

It is very trendy these days to talk about encouraging women to get into tech. But who is this encouragement designed to benefit? Is it for the women? What does it take before industry veterans walk away from the field of work that they love?

If I could take every sexualized moan a woman video-game character produced upon being hit,

> every time a woman dropped out of tech before she got started,

> every time I was mistaken for any other trans woman in games,

every time an indie game developer told a friend of mine she could give him a blowjob,

every time a Mojang security guard refused to reject a sexual assailant from an industry party,

every time a trans woman or person of color was told they were being "too angry,"

every night a woman I know had to spend sleeping at someone else's house because she was afraid of staying at her own,

every time a woman of color was fired for speaking up about harassment,

every scream of every animatronic woman in every David Cage game,

every list of "fake geek girls" or the "forty hottest women in tech,"

every time I've burst into tears because I didn't know how I was going to make rent,

if I could take every nervous breakdown and stack them up, I would build letters a mile high that say "THEY DON'T DESERVE YOU."

I was doxxed recently, as part of an ongoing campaign of harassment against women in games—you know, the one that never, ever ends. Someone posted my birth name, my partner's birth name, my parents' names and professions, my sisters' names. They posted links to a porn shoot I was in (under my own name, the same name I attach to all of my work), lest there be any doubt that the motivation behind their campaign is anything other than punishing women for their sexuality.

The week that happened, I was speaking at a zine festival, to a room full of women, people of color, queer people. I, who have made a career out of encouraging marginalized people to get excited about games, to carve a space for themselves in games culture, I did not feel I could truthfully tell the beautiful people in that room to subject themselves to the ugliness that exists for marginalized people in games. I could not ask them to accept that abuse.

"If they're this mad at you," (we tell each other) "you must be doing something right." In truth, all we're doing is continuing to put up with it—no less than a Herculean task. God, we must be *amazons*.

We must really love FIELD OF WORK. Women in FIELD OF WORK journalism must really care about FIELD OF WORK to put up with the constant abuse, threats, attempts at manipulating their sexual history to get them fired or discredited. Especially when they're *good writers*, they can make way more money and deal with way, way less harassment writing about literally anything else. Especially when their own editors give in to the misogynist children attempting to use their sexuality against them. They must really be passionate about FIELD OF WORK.

Passion is the greatest weakness of anyone in games or tech; it is the thing that will be used against you, time and time again, to wring more unpaid work out of you, to pull you back in again and again. Passion is the reason a poisonous like crunch time is still allowed to exist—a thing that is literally killing and destroying game developers. If you're really passionate about games, you'll do what you have to. Passion is why people in tech voluntarily invent new ways for corporations to mistreat them. Now, thanks to Soylent(TM), we don't even have to feed our employees! We wouldn't want to interrupt your passion for coding with something like food and a momentary break from the endless labor you volunteer for, again and again.

I'm calling for an end to Passion.

"It's a good thing that I love games so much, or—" Stop. *Basta!* There is no "or" anymore. Let's not make it so easy for them.

Games and tech have done nothing to make you feel welcome. They have tried everything they can to hurt you, to wound you. Sisters and brothers, they don't deserve you.

We admire the strength of women, people of color, queers in enduring all this, in managing, somehow, to make rent month after month. It takes lots of it, great stone mountains of strength that rise higher than the loudest catcall or attempt to slut-shame, higher than the tallest ivory tower of the academic with the career-for-life who tells you to calm down, you're being irrational.

But here is another thing that takes strength: to say "No more." To walk away, to choose something else, to protect yourself. To say "I don't deserve this." The strength to unchain yourself from the altar of martyrdom. There's no shame in taking your hand off of something poison.

But anna, what if that's just giving them what they want, though? What if that's just conceding space to them, when we should be maintaining visibility at all costs? What if things are getting better—just very slowly?

What if it's killing you?

THE OTHER SIDE OF DIVERSITY

Erica Joy

So many of our conversations about diversity in tech are from the corporate point of view. We talk about how beneficial minorities are for companies; how diverse teams outperform and about the benefits of diverse perspectives. Such empathy for the needs of Google, Twitter and Dropbox!

What's left out of these conversations is what "diversity" is like for the individuals bringing that difference in color, gender, or sexuality. Erica Joy's essay is a powerful reminder that diversity is actually about people, people who are not only impacting a white-male ecosystem but being affected in return.

The prevailing narrative surrounding minorities in tech relates to how beneficial employing minorities can be for a company and/or how detrimental the lack of diverse perspectives can be. I've searched for, and have been disappointed to find that few studies have been done on the psychological effects of being a minority in a mostly homogeneous workplace for an extended period of time. (Update: There have been some very recently published studies surrounding this topic. I'm very appreciative of Jake Van Epps for pointing them out to me.) Here I'll try to highlight how it has affected me, as I grew from a young black lady to a black woman in the predominantly white male tech industry.

PAST

> *"In consequence to the practice of tokenism, people from minority groups are assimilated or excluded; some token employees assert themselves as the exceptions to the rule, concerning their minority-group stereotype. Hence, in occupations and professions predominantly practiced by men, women join in misogynist male behaviours; and a minority-group token man or woman might intentionally mask his or her true character, in conformity to the majority group's perception of him or her as "the token employee"—http://en.wikipedia.org/wiki/Tokenism*

I began my career in tech at the age of twenty-one, as a Windows System Administrator for the University of Alaska. I was the only woman on my team and one of a few women in my organization. I was the only black woman, the only black person, on the entire floor. I immediately did not fit in, because I didn't look the part. My coworkers walked on eggshells in my presence, so I did my best to make them feel comfortable around me so that I would be included. I laughed at their terribly racist and sexist jokes, I co-opted their negative attitudes, I began to dress as they did, I brushed it off when they made passes at me. I did everything I could to make them feel like I was one of them, even though I clearly was not.

It worked. I was included. I began getting invited to team lunches. They let me in on the jokes they made about our only other teammate who refused to assimilate and was ultimately ostracized for it. They shared their life experiences with me. I was "one of the guys."

When I left that job and hightailed it across the country to Atlanta, I landed in one of the most diverse workplaces I've experienced to this day: The Home Depot Corporate Headquarters (Store Support Center). THD had diversity nailed. I suspect THD's diverse environment had something to do with being in Atlanta, a city that is 54 percent African-American. It's hard not to be diverse when the local demographics force you to be.

Whatever the cause, in my first role at THD, in Network Operations, I was one of two black women and one of six black people, on a team of about twenty. When I transferred to my second team there, Desktop Support, diversity lightning struck: I was a black woman reporting to another black woman in a technical role. Moreover, our team was predominantly black. I could relate to my teammates without having to conform. I didn't have to be anything different than who I was and I flourished there. I was mostly happy at work, happy with life, happy in general. Ultimately though, the other stresses of working at THD (pay inequity, lack of mobility options) led me to seek work at other companies.

After The Home Depot, I took a position at a lottery/ parimutuel company. I returned to being the only black woman, but the team there wasn't very close knit so everybody did their own thing, did their job, and went home.

In 2006, I took an IT Field Technician job at Google in the Atlanta office. While there were black women in the office there (in sales) I was the only one on my direct team of two. Things between my teammate and I were strained, to say the least. It felt like he had some ideas about me that were based on really terrible stereotypes and wasn't shy about sharing them. This was the only time I've ever experienced overt harassment from a coworker. He'd say things like "Did you get that bruise from your boyfriend beating you?" or "I bet your parents abused you as a child." The comments weren't always that blatant or overt, but they were constant and consistent.

Over time, we ended up hiring three more white guys for our team. I was the odd gender and race out, once again. I participated in the various team building activities with the local and larger team to fit in; I began playing first person shooters (not unlike the episode of

The Office where Jim learns how to play Call of Duty), I went to paintball off-sites (despite the fact that I have nightmares about being shot), and the like. I ignored the false assumptions that I was a single mother. I came to work when I was extremely sick to prove that I was a team player, that I belonged.

The negative micro-aggressions from my first coworker continued and I said nothing until I reached my breaking point. He not so subtly hinted that my connecting with the few other black techs in other offices (who happened to be male) was anything other than professional. That was my last straw. I tried to talk to a female teammate in a different office about the situation. She'd been there longer and was something of a leader. She didn't want to get involved. I went to my manager about the problems, told him that I planned to speak with HR. It was decided that the best way to deal with the "tension" between that coworker and I was for me to transfer to New York, despite my not wanting to move there. I don't believe my manager ever engaged HR about the problems and neither did I. I didn't want to make waves and isolate myself further from the team. I didn't want to be that stereotype, the black woman with a chip on her shoulder. I didn't want to make the rest of my team uncomfortable.

In 2007, I left the city where I felt less like an outsider than anywhere I'd lived previously, left my friends, left my love interest, left my life, and started over in a new city.

On the team in New York, I was once again the only black woman. I did what I thought I had to do to survive in the environment. I once again donned the uniform to fit in. Jeans, "unisex" t-shirt, Timbuk2 messenger bag. I stayed late playing multiplayer Battlefield, I quickly learned a bunch of classic rock songs so I could play Rock Band and Guitar Hero with the team, I don't like beer so I went out to beer taverns and drank water. I remember asking if we could do other outings that didn't include beer and getting voted down. I continued to lose myself for the sake of being included amongst my coworkers. We worked a lot then, so my team became my social life and I never hung out with many others. When I left New York to move to Mountain View, I didn't abandon my life in the way that I did when I left Atlanta. I just put down the life I'd picked up from others.

I arrived in the Bay Area in August of 2008. Being in Silicon Valley has been simultaneously great for my career but bad for me as a person. I've been able to work on multiple different teams and really interesting projects. Unfortunately, my workplace is homogenous and so are my surroundings. I feel different everywhere. I go to work and I stick out like a sore thumb. I have been mistaken for an administrative assistant more than once. I have been asked if I was physical security (despite security wearing very distinctive uniforms). I've gotten passed over for roles I know I could not only perform in, but that I could excel in. Most recently, one such role was hired out to a contractor who needed to learn the language the project was in (which happened to be my strongest language). I spent some time and energy trying to figure out why that happened, if it was to do with unconscious bias or if it was an honest mistake.

Outside of work, I've lived several places in the Bay Area: San Jose, Sunnyvale, Santa Clara, San Bruno. All places I felt like I didn't belong. I walked around and saw scant few other black women. There was nowhere I felt like I could fit in. I spent many nights at home alone, just to avoid feeling different. The worst thing is that it didn't have to be this way.

PRESENT

en-cul-tu-ra-tion

/en, kelCHe'rāSHen/

noun: inculturation; noun: enculturation the gradual acquisition of the characteristics and norms of a culture or group by a person, another culture, etc.

I recently dated a guy who happened to live in Oakland and had severe reservations about going to visit him. In fact, before we began dating, I never visited the East Bay unless I absolutely had to, and always went in the daytime. I always worried that I'd be the victim of some crime. Despite the fact that I grew up spending summers next door to some of the "worst" areas of

Richmond, Virginia, despite the only real friend I had in the Bay Area living there, I was scared to go to the East Bay. Many people were telling me in no uncertain terms that the East Bay was Very Bad. Crime happens there. It's not for Us. Definitely don't live there. The result was that I avoided the one place in the Bay Area I could go and feel not so different. It never dawned on me that the people who were telling me not to go there were the people who might go there and feel uncomfortable. It never dawned on me that I'd let other peoples experiences and cultural upbringing completely negate my own. It never dawned on me that I really wasn't in the set of Us.

When I finally started to visit Oakland regularly, after some initial skittishness, I fell in love with it. I couldn't really put my finger on why until my relationship ended and I went to therapy to figure some things out. I realized that I've been searching for a community for the last thirteen years and have been trying and failing to find that sense of community at work. When I visited Oakland, went to First Friday, walked Lake Merritt, talked to the people at the corner store, that sense of community found me. I felt like I was home. I don't think it's coincidence that I felt that sense of belonging in a place that wasn't so homogeneous. Some part of me felt free to relax and breathe. It was ok to be me, there was nobody I had to make comfortable with my existence.

Being in therapy has forced me to process my emotions, to understand what is going on in the background cycles of my mind. This has helped to identify exactly what effect being a black woman in tech, being the outlier for thirteen years, has had on me. For those who like bullet points, I'll provide those here:

- I feel alone every day I come to work, despite being surrounded by people, which results in feelings of isolation.
- I feel like I stick out like sore thumb every day.
- I am constantly making micro-evaluations about whether or not my actions will be attributed to my being "different."
- I feel like my presence makes others uncomfortable so I try to make them feel comfortable.
- I feel like there isn't anyone who can identify with my story, so I don't tell it.
- I feel like I have to walk a tightrope to avoid reinforcing stereotypes while still being heard.
- I have to navigate the expectation of stereotypical behavior and disappointment when it doesn't happen (e. g. my not being the "sassy black woman").
- I frequently wonder how my race and gender are coloring perceptions of me.
- I wonder if and when I've encountered racists (the numbers say it's almost guaranteed that I have) and whether or not they've had an effect on my career.
- I feel a constant low level of stress every day, just by virtue of existing in my environment.

- I feel like I've lost my entire cultural identity in effort to be part of the culture I've spent the majority of the last decade in.

The stress and isolation I mentioned have really taken their toll on me. Long term stress is known to cause health issues. Not long after I started working in New York, I developed heart problems (PVC's). About three years ago I started to get acne, something I've never had in my life. I always thought it was hormonal but now recognize that it happens when I'm stressed. The isolation and resultant loneliness have exacerbated the stress, leaving me in constant fight or flight mode. Running hasn't been an option, so I would argue with people for no reason at all, because the long term stress made every interaction a fight. The stress also caused some level of depression, which I wasn't really aware of until recently.

I'm working on fixing this, for the sake of my mental and physical health. Ideally I'd like to work in a less homogenous environment where I don't feel so different. Instead, I'm focusing on modifying my life outside of work and reducing the time I spend at work. I'm moving to the East Bay as soon as my lease is up, so that I have a respite from the homogeneity and I can have a chance to relax. I'm signing up for every MeetUp that is relevant to me that involves other black women. I'm volunteering with organizations that will help the younger generation get involved in tech, so we can change the ratio (Black Girls Code, Hack The Hood) and those who come after me won't have to feel how I've felt. I've stopped trying to assimilate at work. I'm no longer trying to make people comfortable with my existence. I am trying to connect with other black women in technical roles. I'm standing up for what I believe in and standing up for myself, instead of sitting quietly by, so as not to not make waves.

Most importantly I am working on re-establishing my authentic self. This process is scary and difficult and will take some time and work. I have to search through myself and figure out what characteristics I've dropped in order to fit in. I have to sift through my personality and pick out the bits that aren't really me. I have to understand who I am without the detritus of the habits and behaviors I've picked up while trying to assimilate.

I know this: I am not my job. I am not my industry or its stereotypes. I am a black woman who happens to work in the tech industry. I don't need to change to fit within my industry. My industry needs to change to make everyone feel included and accepted.

LESBIANS WHO TECH

Leanne Pittsford

Lesbians face unique challenges in corporate culture. LGBTQ women also face different issues than LGBTQ men. Gay men earn higher incomes than gay women, and lesbians households are more likely to have children— just for starters.

I've been attending Leanne Pittsford's "Lesbians Who Tech" summits since 2014. These events are inclusive (allies welcome) in case any Lean Out *readers are intrigued. Of all the tech conferences I've attended, these summits are my favorite. Warm and welcoming, and yet completely professional, I like to imagine other industry events someday having a similar vibe.*

Queer women in tech is a different experience from women in tech. There is an added dimension straight women do not have to deal with. Take for e.g. the name of this book *Lean Out*; it perfectly captures what *Lean In* missed. While the latter was an important step toward elevating the discussion of gender in tech, it primarily captured the straight woman's perspective. It's important for all women to be visible and heard, to share stories and experiences. Lesbians Who Tech provides a platform for queer women to do just that.

As queer women, how many times have we walked into an LGBTQ event with optimism and a sense of community but left feeling disappointed and without any successful connections or meaningful conversations? I can't be the only one with this experience. And I've had a lot of them.

The last decade has led me to work with the gay and lesbian community in various ways. Having studied equity and social justice in graduate school, I made sure the work I was involved with reflected those principles. I had a staff position at Equality California where I did a lot of work around Prop 8, a role as a board member at a nonprofit and ran a mentoring program for lesbian entrepreneurs. I'm sure the work I did made some impact, some difference, but I could not ignore the glaring lack of engagement and, in some ways, understanding, organizations and groups had when it came to queer women. I still wonder why gender equality has been left off the gay agenda.

Over and over I saw LGBTQ communities and organizations miss the mark. And after spending three years in Silicon Valley, I saw an even more specific underserved market—LGBTQ women in tech. Women in Silicon Valley had their own set of challenges but gay women had an added layer to overcome. If women make less than men, even more so in tech, then lesbian couples have a much bigger economic gap than straight couples and double that of gay men. While there were women-centered events and LGBTQ events, there was nothing tailored specifically for LGBTQ women in tech. I wasn't able to fix this problem within a larger structure so I decided to go out on my own.

Why have such a focused group like Lesbians Who Tech? Because there was a need. However seemingly silent and unseeing, there was a huge gaping need.

It can be frustrating to deal with representation issues within the LGBTQ community.

Ever been to an event where 70 to 90 percent of the attendees were gay men and/or male allies? I have. It's a little absurd to think that using the umbrella of 'LGBTQ' is sufficient enough to address issues within the group when representation is so skewed. There is nothing wrong with gay men getting together and creating a space for themselves but call it what it is, let's not pretend that these events actively seek to engage queer women in tech. They may try but I really don't think they try hard enough. This is not an "us vs. them" issue. I saw a need to create Lesbians Who Tech because there wasn't a space for us like this before.

I got equal flack from LGBTQ and women's groups when I first discussed the idea. And I'll admit it, I was one of those people (back in my nonprofit days) who would ask "Why all the alliances and coalition meetings, why couldn't we just have one big group?" I realized soon enough that for a community to have a voice, organizing from that said community was important. That ensures a voice—and makes sure that voice is heard. Also, it's about access points; the easier we make our entry points for people, the more effective the impact.

It all started fairly simple: happy hour in San Francisco. Because of my own personal experiences I thought it would be interesting to experiment with my queer friends in tech and see if they were feeling the same way. The reason for the experimental fashion was because I really wanted to make sure that there was a community out there that wanted specific value and was different from the other women-focused groups that already existed.

We really wanted to build an actual community.

On a chilly December evening in 2012, we held our first happy hour with over forty people in attendance. And two months later that number grew to a hundred. Nine months into this experiment it was clear to me that queer women in tech wanted a space where we could openly be ourselves and yet be in a professional environment where conversations would not be limited to just our sexual identities, and actually start from a place of connecting professionally first. This was the strong feedback I got—that most of the women in Lesbians Who Tech said that they finally found a place where they felt they were welcomed and felt comfortable. Focusing on tech first allowed them to bring their whole self to the conversation.

I spoke with people who attended the events and found out that while they enjoyed the happy hours, they wanted more tech-related events and more visible role models from the community. When I asked them to name high profile lesbians (or any for that matter) in tech, many could not name one. That's when I realized the value I could provide in making this group really mean something and to go to the next level. And that's how the Lesbians Who Tech summit came to be in February of 2014. I was expecting about 300 but over 800 queer women in tech showed up (and allies). We had 30 queer women speakers and 30 percent women of color. It was a tech event where queer women led conversations. A few months later in June we had friends from the east coast organize a NYC summit, they had 400 people in attendance.

Countless queer women came up to me after the summit and expressed how encouraged, inspired, and validated they were. The summit provided visibility to a group in tech that has been somewhat faceless. Many queer women said that to see role models and big time names in Silicon Valley like Megan Smith, Kara Swisher, Jana Rich, and Sara Sperling, among others, was ground-breaking. They had never seen anyone on stage talk about experiences they shared. They felt a deep connection and a sense of true community. Maybe that's why Lesbians Who Tech 's membership is over 9,000 now.

And then the White House called. We were asked to co-organize the first ever LGBT Tech and Innovation Summit there. We brought in organizations and people in our community from across the country to talk about the intersection of technology and support for crucial work that's happening and still needs to be done in the LGBTQ community. We made sure there was a 50/50 split among women/men, with lots of representation among men and women of color and the transgender community.

And in February of 2015 we sold out our second San Francisco Summit with over 1,200 women and allies. Queer women took over the Castro district, a neighborhood dominated by gay men, in a way that's never been done before. We held conversations in bars, gave our first award to Megan Smith, the Chief Technology Officer of the United States and asked Kara Swisher to hold a conversation with Marc Benioff, the Chairman and CEO of Salesforce.com around diversity in technology. It's important to note this community and energy would not exist without thousands of queer women and allies showing up for themselves and for their community. The three leaders are a great example of both.

There are big plans for Lesbians Who Tech. It still blows my mind that we've done events in twenty-two cities, and that some of those were held internationally. I've quit everything to do this full-time because I see the value it provides. I've also had tremendous help from amazing volunteers who are just as passionate about this cause. Part of my plan is to go on a listening tour from the west coast to the east coast called #WeAreTech, bringing together all the amazing organizations who are working toward increasing representation in technology to showcase the incredible and unique stories in technology. We're thinking about a one day shadow career program called "Bring a Lesbian to Work Day," sustainability, scale, scholarship funds for people to learn how to code, and so much more.

Ultimately our main goal is to raise the profile, the stories, the visibility of people in our community and the amazing things they are doing. We want to nurture the next generation of upcoming leaders, to give a platform for people to speak, and provide a space that was non-existent just over two years ago. And I know when we do that we'll inspire the next generation of queer women to take the technology industry by storm.

WHAT YOUNG WOMEN IN TECH REALLY NEED

Jenni Lee

The landscape of Silicon Valley is changing to include more awareness of diversity. We're seeing companies like Google and Facebook hosting events just for women. What we aren't seeing is women, LGTBQ and people of color being given equal stage time where it matters—in the board room, at promotion time, and with signed term sheets for founders.

Jenni Lee, a brilliant young startup entrepreneur, tells us straight up "What Young Women in Tech Really Need."

I was talking to a friend from college about her job search—a dreary topic for many college soon-to-be grads. She's a dual computer science and economics minor. She's smart like that. She was lamenting about how she had gotten several interviews at prestigious tech firms like Google, but all they really wanted to do was parade her in front of their "See! We support women in tech" conferences and marketing campaigns.

"They like to show me off to the crowd and tease me by giving me one interview, but then they just funnel me off to the next women in tech conference and I'm like, 'I need a job, not another conference,'" she says.

So here's my message: hey Google, thanks but your effort to bring more women into tech is really just tokenism. Instead of throwing money at the problem (i.e. paying for a few women to take coding classes or putting them up in nice hotels at women's only conferences), you should just give them a dignified job. Put your money where your PR is.

Given all the talk in the press and social media posts about supporting women in tech, you would expect there to be actual support. But in reality, it's an uphill battle even to get introductions.

I reached out to my social and professional networks recently, asking for career help and asking to be connected to so and so. I had just accepted a position as Marketing Manager at Statisfy, a startup focused on a question and answering platform. Many of my closest and most-trusted mentors had my back, including the very inspiring JoAnne Kennedy (whom I met via Twitter of all places!). They gave me advice, connected me to people who could help me, and encouraged me to push harder. That being said, there were a surprising number of supposed mentors who not only denied me help but claimed that I was being "over-promotional" and hungry.

Admittedly, I am a direct person and I ask for what I want. But these comments really gave me pause. If I were a young man pitching and asking for help in a friendly professional setting, would I get a different response? Would I be lauded for my tactful aggressiveness and be crowned as business savvy? The answer, I believe, is yes. Business, most notably tech, suffers from the same problems as politics wherein aggressive women are labeled as "bitchy," and aggressive men are praised as "leaders."

To Google and other mega tech companies, I say this: young women like me don't need another feel-good, ego-massage Google program. To the supposed women-in-tech advocates and the feminists, I say this: we welcome your help, but we need more than just encouraging words.

As a young woman just beginning her career in tech, I can tell you what young women in tech like me need:

- *Networks and introductions:* If men have old boys clubs, why can't women form the same type of professional and social networks as well? Why can't we connect one another for professional gains and reasons? Is it inherently selfish and self-serving to want to ask to be introduced to so-and-so? Maybe. But that is not the point. If we are going to be competitive for the same jobs, in the same world as men, we need to start taking each other and our social capital seriously. We need to mine and use each other, kindly of course, but utilize each other and each other's resources nonetheless. If resources aren't being used, what are they good for? A lot of business today is still conducted in quasi-professional settings with a lot of personal and inter-network introductions. In order to build our network, especially as young women, we need mentors and our peers to create and expand our networks. Together, we can create an army of women in tech who are unstoppable and generous in accepting and helping new group members. The best part? When one of us succeeds, we all do. And we all feel that same shared sense of pride because after all, it takes a village.

- *Mentorship:* This is perhaps the most important need. Instead of sending us to free coding classes (thanks, Google) or giving over-generalized advice, how about women techies (who are in a position to help) extending a hand to us young ones? I promise we'll listen. A mentor, especially a mentor in a profession, is like another parent. They guide you, look out for your best interests, and tailor their knowledge and messages to your circumstance. And best of all? Both mentor and mentee experience a deep bond and a sense of togetherness that is rare in this digital day and age.

- Stop shaming or discouraging us for being "over promotional." Many non-tech women have accused me of being "not sensitive" or "over promotional." To you, I say this: "How dare you try to quell my fire, especially with nonsensical sexist psychology!" I mean every word of that. Do I strive to be perfect? No, and I'm happy with my flawless flaws, thank you very much. Do I strive to well-liked by everyone? Certainly not. That ship has long sailed. So I have a proposal: how about instead of discouraging young women from doing what is *necessary* for career success, why don't we encourage them and send them our support (and networks!)? I promise you there is only bubbly proud-mama-bear feelings ahead. Lastly, I'd like to point out that young men are not nearly as often labeled as *over* promotional or "self serving" as young women are in assertive business behavior. Why is this? There are lots of reasons, but I'll just point out one: we have two different standards for young men and women. When a guy is pushing his agenda or being "business-like," he is lauded as a "great talent" or future CEO. When a woman is doing the same thing, we tell her to be quiet, and that she is over promotional or some form of "selfish." Bleh. Politics has the same problem: an assertive man is a "great leader" and an assertive woman is a "bitch." Are we not allowed to pursue the same intentions and dreams as our male counter-parts? I'm #sorrynotsorry if my gender offends your ideas of what women *should* be like.

As for Google, you can teach a man to fish—but what if they're not welcome at the pond?

That's what comes to mind when I think about Google and their "we'll send women to coding classes!"

marketing campaign. At first, when I heard about the Google voucher program, I thought, "Great! They're changing their tune and really rolling up their sleeves to commit to *real* change." Then, when I step back and look at the bigger picture and the aftermath of the "we'll send women to coding school" campaign, part of my soul cringes. Why? For one, Google may be teaching a few select women how to code (or at least sending them to the right places), but they are not providing a pond for the women to practice their new fishing skills (or in this case, coding skills). In other words, Google may be teaching women how to code, but they are not providing an opportunity for women to use, sharpen, and try out those skills. That is one of the biggest reasons why I decided to stay in startup land and to stick with Statisfy, my current company. I'm no coder, but I can tell you that my current company (and many other startups I've worked in) put their money where their mouth is. Instead of saying, "*Of course* we support women in leadership positions in tech firms," I want to see more of "*See!* We've actually put women in leadership positions because we see their potential." I'd like to see fewer talking heads and fair-weather tech campaigns. I'd also like to see supposed female as well as male feminist advocates step up and *show* us [young women] support. Don't soft play us: we can take it just as much as the boys can. I promise. We're the next generation of movers and shakers, but without mentors and the active support of our allies, it's going to be an unnecessarily difficult and lonely road ahead.

RUNNERS
Ash Huang

It's clear that climbing the corporate ladder isn't a one-size-fits-all approach. It's not for everyone. Making a home for yourself at Google or Dropbox HQ isn't only about cultural fit along gender lines. Like Ash, I find open office plans to be a version of hell. That has nothing to do with my gender, and everything to do with my introversion. Of course, there are plenty of gender-related reasons to avoid office politics.

Ash represents, for me, someone who has found a better way. When I think about what it means to "lean out," I think of people like her. What is feminism for, if not encouraging women to use our freedoms to choose the paths that suit us? Good feminist, bad feminist—Ash is a doing-it-her-way feminist. And I think that's one of the very best kinds.

I always seem to be lying on the couch when I read status updates from my runner friends. As I scroll through photos of their medals, their easy conquests of the Himalayas and other absurd mountains, I have to pat myself on the shoulder. There, there. If you worked hard and favored exercise that didn't incorporate chanting and slow stretching, you, too could win races. You, too, could make backroom deals with Greek goddesses and mock the known limits of the human body.

I'm not built to be an athlete. I'm short, incredibly near-sighted, and have been known to slip on banana peels in parking lots. But people love a good underdog story. Deciding to rise when the fates would have you fail is the ultimate human romance. Imagine the clickbait if I went full Rocky for a year.

How a short, incredibly near-sighted tech worker went from couch potato to ripped in just twelve months!

Impressive. However, if you told me that today was the day that I'd have to run a hundred miles, I would not be ready. There'd be no scenes of me on the steps with my boxing gloves in the air. There'd probably just be a coffin and lots of flowers, *Fin* scripted across the screen.

Our long tradition of stories is based on facing adversity. Facing an institution, a villain, or even just yourself. We root for underdogs because we know that personal adversity drives change. Humans are special because we insist on battling impossible odds.

Unfortunately, we don't often get to choose what adversity we draw from the stack, nor when. We don't choose what color our skin is or what parts hang in our underpants. We don't choose which of our family members get hit with cancer or whose eyes go milky with glaucoma.

When we're not prepared for adversity, the odds dwindle and the romance often fades.

This randomness can make us forget that we do control some things. We can choose to go cliff diving or learn a new language. We can seek out and select some of the adversity in our life. This is also a part of being human.

We can pick where we work. The cynics will disagree and say that beggars can't be choosers. That we must tolerate difficult environments and dodge constant sabotage. This is a lie. It's a simplification of a complex world. Most things are possible, it's more a question of what is wise.

Wisdom is deeply personal. If it were one size fits all, we would have many more wise nineteen-year-olds. We'd have a book we could crack open and mine for solutions. Wisdom comes not from finding the road, but from knowing yourself well enough that you understand how to live in your own universe. The wise know how to interface with other humans in a productive way and how to do good work in an upstanding manner.

Individual wisdom applies deeply to equality. Many choose to fight sexist workplaces from the inside. They fight from within for better maternity and paternity rights, parking spaces for imminent mothers, consequences for sexual harassment and proper management training.

This is not the path that I chose. I left that world with no regrets because change is never made in just one way.

We need public protest, we need laws put into action, we need teachers to reprimand bullies, we need actresses to gravitate toward strong female leads. Change is not a single series of boxes we check off and forget. It is a constant battle from a thousand fronts fought by a thousand different types.

My fight isn't destined to be at just one company right now. Though I can be chatty, I am excruciatingly introverted. I have little interest in managing people. I'd much rather spend my time as an individual contributor and hone my craft. Plus, the startup open office plan is my version of hell on Earth.

When I stopped working as a fulltime in-house designer, a few flat-out accused me of being a weak feminist and running away. It's crazy that there's even this idea of being a "bad feminist," or that one should do feminism the "right" way. It's deeply ironic to fight for choice and agency for women while demanding they bear only one sort of battle scar.

Sure. I ran away. That's because in order to run toward something, you must inevitably run away from something else. In that moment, I understood what I needed. I saw a better way for me to shape tools that help humans. I could do it without deleting myself in favor of someone else's path.

How to Run Away

My ideal job is not everyone's ideal job. Regardless, my job freedom has three pillars: people, work and money.

Money

Unfortunately money and budgets are a major roadblock to feeling secure in a new career or a new job environment. People who tell you that you're above money are either loaded or optimistically delusional. Smile and nod at them.

Working for people means you owe people things in return for money. If you're financially solvent, you can be much pickier about which people you owe things to.

Enough people have written about how to budget that I'll leave you to Google it. Only: spend less than you make and stash money in retirement funds (if you aren't already). Through IRS magic, it often means that you pay much less in taxes and keep that money for later.

People

Traditional wisdom cites "networking" as an act of quick impression. Many send crazy calling cards and wait for the flies to land in the honeytrap. There's a reason people roll their eyes at "networking." It's often not genuine.

The way to find good people is not to charm legions, but rather to find individuals who throw off complimentary vibes to yours. It's easy to get caught up in the hairy world of "networking," but in a community like tech it's about finding brethren. As much as any of us might harp on balance and maintaining other interests, it's fun to talk shop. We derive great joy from geeking out on beautiful logos, elegant syntax, or weird new machines.

Be patient and curious. Your people are life-long relationships. Sometimes you'll have an opportunity, sometimes they'll have an opportunity. Mostly you'll just want to get nerdy. A large majority of the interesting projects that pop up in my inbox are intros from friends I've known for years. We are simple creatures and it feels good to help. When two friends are introduced and make awesome stuff together, we can't help but smile a little and think, "I did that. Mu-ha-ha."

It's corny, sure. Finding and enjoying other people is also the only way to really have a "network."

Work

Aim to do good work. Seek out jobs with discerning teams and opportunities that fascinate you. Never confuse status and bragging rights for quality of work. Working at a place people have actually heard of is great for your career. I strove to do this and I had fun. But if you're ever fortunate enough to do so and you don't like what you're making, you'll feel like the biggest fraud in the nation. At cocktail parties everyone will surmise how grateful you must be and your insides will go dark.

As you get to know people in the industry and can afford rent and real food, take objective looks at your work. I look at my work at the beginning of each month and ask myself: what's lacking? What was rewarding because it helped people and moved them, rather than what I was rewarded for? What got in the way? Did it have to get in the way? What did I really love to do? Write it down if you have to.

On the Treadmill

As a part of my training to be a fulfilled and happy human, there are things I consciously do and don't do anymore.

I Work Independently

When people pay you for discrete gigs, it turns out they usually want to define exactly what you owe them. I don't have to do the murky stuff that women don't get paid extra for in full-time jobs: extra recruiting/interviews so there's always a woman in the interview loop, playing diplomat to people who don't think sexism exists, fighting to get more women hired. Instead I do these on my own terms and I don't walk on eggshells. I can call out generalized bad behavior without worrying about hurting a company.

Someday this might not serve me anymore. I might find a company that has an irresistible team and mission. For now, I'm happy to help others, improve my work and examine the industry on my own.

I Admit Confusion to Myself

I was fortunate enough to know that I wanted to be a designer at eighteen. Other things have not been so clear. Sometimes the answer to what I want or what's true is, "I don't know." In these situations I do not consider myself lost. Rather, I test it out. An example:

I asked myself whether I enjoyed working with big teams on specific projects or with young startups on whatever chaos came their way. I didn't know. So I spent last year working with a range of teams. It turns out that my question is sort of invalid. I like working with some big teams and some young startups. The team ethos and problems trump any structure, and the variety is important to me.

We can try to feign omniscience or we can admit a fork in the road. The humble latter might mean turning back once or twice, but you'll be surer of where you're heading in the end.

I Don't Do Everything

Perfection is the enemy, particularly for women who are told from childhood that they must be flawless. While boys are chasing frogs and eating mudpies, girls are told to be ladylike. We live in a society where "women have to be twice as good as men" is a cheeky mantra spouted with an aw shucks grin. Men wander the streets without moisturizing while women are afraid to leave the house without eyeliner, mascara, and a nice bright lip.

So I don't value personal perfection. I don't have to be the most badass visual designer, product thinker, product manager, front end ninja and marketer all in one. I've picked six kinds of design and strategy that I concentrate on with clients. It makes it much easier to say no to jobs I haven't enjoyed as much in the past and puts my focus back on learning. This might sound counterintuitive, but it's because of the learning curve.

When you learn a skill you know nothing of, going from super terrible to kind of terrible is a more obvious difference than going from expert to guru. Right now I'd like to explore more subtle expertise, so I'm working on that.

I Don't Internalize Mistakes as Character Flaws

Everyone makes mistakes. You can define yourself as a mistake maker or a person who made a mistake. There are instances where you can't afford to make mistakes, but those situations are reserved for situations of life and death.

Blame is not a useful thing. Understanding a situation and learning is the only way to move forward. Even if you work with people who blame you when things go wrong, you cannot take all responsibility for everything. To do so is a sad form of narcissism—all of the baggage, none of the perks.

Have Your Rocky Moment. Get Up Again and Do Better

I don't laugh nervously when people say careless things.

This is one I learned from the trolls. When someone makes a racist comment or sweeps someone into stereotype, I ask that person to explain the joke to me. For instance:

A laughing group of random blonde women cross the street in SOMA. A man I'm with says in falsetto: "Ha ha ha, look at us, marketing is like, totally the best!"

Me: "Oh, they're in marketing? How do you know them? Are they old co-workers of yours?"

Trolling carelessness works because this kind of injustice thrives on community. People are blindly intolerant because they are rewarded for shunning and fearing the Other. When you refuse to participate in a universe where women are weak and inconsequential, women become more than a generalization. The shared joke is no longer funny because there's no more shared joke to speak of.

I Don't Ask If It's Okay

Throughout my adult life, I was rewarded for being sweet. Co-workers would comment on my "cute," petite size and say that I was a team player. If you want to watch someone flip from warm to cold in an instant, offer a conflicting viewpoint after being deemed sweet.

I noticed a few years ago that the emails I wrote were vastly different from the emails my boyfriend or male friends would write. Mine were filled with excessive emoji (__("J)_/_), exclamation marks (!!!!!!!), can we's and what do you think's. I would agonize over a single email, hoping that the recipient wouldn't think me cold or abrupt. I would have ideas of what was the best path forward, but I would present them in a way that whoever was on the other end would actually be the decisionmaker, not me.

I sometimes keep the emoji and exclamation marks because it's actually how I talk, but I don't ask for decisions as often. Especially being a hired gun, I'm expected to make recommendations for clients. Where I would have presented information in the past and then said, should we x, I now say, based on this info, x could be effective.

It's not just big things, though. I've applied this to pricing, scheduling, and priorities. Instead of saying, this week I was thinking of making style guides for the Android app, what do you think about that, I'll say: this week I'm going to make style guides for the Android app. If something is higher priority, let me know.

There's an out given, but it wasn't given by asking permission.

A word of caution: there are people out there who will unconsciously dislike a woman who doesn't ask. This is a huge red flag. Even in a junior position, the expectation at a quality company is that you will grow to be a contributing member of the team. As people who work, we are tasked with gathering information and then figuring out options for how to proceed. Good leaders double check for hazardous gaps in knowledge and leave decision-making to the people who are doing the work. Demanding an informed adult human person to ask teacher for final permission is infantilization.

The Marathon
I left full-time work disillusioned with the state of Silicon Valley. Instead of burrowing me deeper into that sorrow, working with clients has made me an optimist. The potential for tech to do great things for the world is real. I'm heartened by the clients I meet who love their

users, strive to make a difference and treat their team with respect.

It's easy to become a cynic when you're down at work. It can seem like there are only a few alternatives: learn not to care, fight tooth and nail to be heard, or quit. Women are leaving tech in droves because of this limited tree of options.

I want you to know: there are good people out there who do see women as equal or are learning how. They may not yet be a majority, but they are a growing sect. If fighting from the inside is not your game, you can make a difference by voting with your feet. You can choose to align your talents with people who will help you grow and challenge you productively.

There are a thousand ways to carry a revolution. It's only a matter of finding your way home.

BREAKING THE BRO CODE
Dom DeGuzman

I am inspired by Dom because she has figured out how to navigate tech culture, and made such a good home for herself at Twilio. She knows how to succeed and be happy in tech—and shares her experiences in a way that makes you feel like you can do it too.

The first time I spoke about brogrammers on stage, a woman approached me with tears in her eyes and told me that I'd put the last twenty years of her career into words. Since then I have traveled the globe talking about my relationship with brogrammers and I've learned that this story, my story, was no longer my story but a shared experience.

My name is Dom and I am currently a software engineer at Twilio. I focus on infrastructure monitoring,

development tools, and the general engineering platform. I like to describe my job as maintaining engineering
headaches. Along with development, I am also one of
the founding members of the diversity and inclusion
program, and a San Francisco City director for Lesbians Who Tech. Before I continue, I want to point out
that this is a compilation of stories from various companies and teams I had been a part of. These stories don't
reflect my time at Twilio, which has been a warm and
supportive environment for me.

Let's start with my background and how I came to
where I am now. I am not one of those people that knew
exactly what I wanted to do with my life. My career has
never been linear. I don't even have a background in
STEM. In fact, the main reason I went to college was
because I thought that was what I was supposed to do.
While most college freshmen are undeclared majors,
I remained undeclared most of my college career.
I focused more on my social life than I did on focusing
on a major. I would follow my friends into their classes
or wander into a classroom and just stay if I became
interested. It didn't matter if I was enrolled or if it were
halfway through a semester; I would stay and participate out of raw curiosity. I took college as an opportunity to learn whatever it was I wanted to learn and as
an excuse to put off growing up. This is how I ended
up with a transcript that includes Sexualities in Communication, Black Sexual Politics, Broadcasting, Come-
dic Script Writing, Gay & Lesbian History, Women's

Studies, Philosophy of Modern Television, Pop American Culture, Growth Through Adventure, Performative Arts, Modern Rhetoric and many many other seemingly unrelated classes.

After about seven years, the dean pulled me into her office and told me that I needed to get it together and graduate. Since my classes were so scattered across multiple disciplines, I was able to petition for a "Special Major" where I wrote a central thesis in what I've learned over my time resulting in my official degree being a communication analysis of the heteronormativity within lesbians and lesbian relationships within mainstream media.

Instead, many employers found that my "special degree" meant that I was unfocused and could not follow guidelines or rules. At one point during this employment search I worked at a chain electronic store selling computers. If you told me then that I was going to be where I am now, I would have laughed and probably tried to sell you a Compaq computer.

I turned selling computers into fixing home computers. I turned that into fixing computers at an enterprise level, which led to fixing enterprise Linux software. That led me into writing code and becoming a professional software developer. This was not an easy journey and not having a degree or formalized background in computer science did not work in my favor. While I was learning and adapting to my new career paths, there was one group of people who always made it a steeper uphill battle for me: The Brogrammers.

Let's start off with a simplified definition of the brogrammer. Traditionally speaking, the technical industry
has been dominated by not only men, but introverted,
socially awkward men. But now, with the technical industry boom, that has all changed. Now, the frat boys you
thought you left in college have packed up their flip
flops and shitty beer and moved into the desks next to
you. The men that used to flood into finance, sales, and
business are now "crushing it in Ruby" and playing beer
pong between deployments. This is not only shifting the
dynamic and culture of the tech industries but they are
beginning to shape it as well. This is largely responsible
for incredibly sexist and misogynistic events like "Hackers and Hookers" or presentations like "Maven is my
girlfriend," not to mention the prevalence of recruiting
events held at places like whiskey and cigar bars.

I'm born and raised in the Bay Area, and have
watched the rise of the brogrammers in the San Francisco
tech industry. I've identified five very distinct stages I
would go through every time I've had to work with a new
set of brogrammers.

The First Stage Being, Denial

Now there are two types of denial; the denial of skillset
and the denial of sexuality. Brogrammers would always
find some excuse for why I wasn't good enough to be
trusted with larger projects. Whether it was because I
was younger, a female, not from the Ivy League or didn't
have a degree in computer science, there was always

some reason that a brogrammer would look over my shoulder to make sure I was doing something correctly.

The second type of denial is the denial of sexuality. Now, this is a little different from the type of denial that lesbians who have come before me have had to face. Nobody asked me to stay closeted; in fact it was almost the opposite. Brogrammers like to think of themselves as forward thinking and accepting. I can't tell you how many times I would hear "I dated a bi girl once" as a means of trying to find common ground. I don't care that you've dated a bi girl. But what I've found is that brogrammers would rather treat me as *one of the guys* rather than acknowledge me as a queer woman. This would include asking me to participate in judging and rating women or indulging in intimate details of a relationship. As much as I wanted to respond with, "shut up before I replace you with a 13 line Bash script" my more suitable response was, "I'm sorry, we may both *like* women, but I actually respect them."

The Next Stage is Anger

There are times I wanted to scream about how much I hated working with brogrammers. This isn't the anger I am talking about. The anger I am referring to isn't something that is outright. It isn't something you notice right away. It's an anger that slowly builds inside of you. In my case, the two biggest contributors to my deep and slow burning anger are the allowance of too many little things ("death by a thousand paper cuts") and persistent, unwelcome, brogrammer commentary.

There are moments when you hear things that will make your jaw clench and muscles tense. It may be a rape joke, a gay joke, a genitals joke, or being in a windowless room of farts. They are things that will make you annoyed and almost mad, but you don't bring it up. You think it's not worth the tension or potential aftermath. You think that your anger is really just a temporary feeling of annoyance, and that it will pass. It doesn't pass. It builds. As you keep this anger inside, you don't notice how toxic it becomes. It seeps into your relationships with your colleagues and affects your ability to work productively.

The second is unwelcomed brogrammer commentary. A brogrammer colleague and I were once up for the same promotion. We had the same amount of experience and skillset but I had a college degree and he didn't. After I got the promotion, we went out to drinks to celebrate. One drink in and he told me that I really deserved the promotion. Jump ahead a few drinks and he told me that I got the promotion because I was a "hat trick." Taken aback, I asked him to clarify what he meant. He repeated, "hat trick. Like in hockey when you score three points in a row." First, just because I am gay doesn't mean that I understand sports references. Second, he meant that because I was a woman, a person of color, and because I was queer that I would be considered a diversity goldmine. He wanted me to feel bad that he was having a hard time moving up in the company because he was a straight, white man and there was nothing unique about it. What's worse is that he thought he was complimenting me by telling me that I was guaranteed work because of who I was, and not because of my skillset.

I want to set something very clear here. I got to where I am because I worked really hard and I am good at what I do; it has nothing to do with filling a quota.

Moving on, The Next Stage is Bargaining

Bargaining is what happens when you let the little things pass. When you feel your blood boil but let it go, that is the first step of becoming one of them. When you are on a team (and it doesn't matter if they are brogrammers or not) you do want that sense of being a part of that group. You don't want to feel like the outsider in a group of friends or coworkers. So you'll start hanging out after work. You'll participate in a little chat about something you barely care about, like cars or sports or Meghan Fox, and it grows from there. I became a brogrammer. I bought Beats Headphones and listened to Mac Miller. I gave the best high fives and played wing woman at the bars. And though I felt closer to my team, I felt further and further away from who I really was.

Predictably, The Next Stage is Depression

Not being true to who I was, pretending I was infiltrating when really I was conforming, left me upset at myself. I was unhappy with my workplace. I wasn't happy hearing penis jokes and only drinking gross watery beer. It began to show in my work. I stopped going the extra mile and only churned out tickets as they came to me because I didn't want to spend more time in the office than I had to. My partner would call me out on not being authentic and she was right.

You would think that the next stage is acceptance, but it's really not. See, I don't want anyone to think that you should just accept being unhappy in the workplace, I don't want that to be seen as okay. Acceptance should NOT be the final stage.

Maybe there is no final stage. If you want to work where brogrammers work, you have to learn to work with them and still be your true, most authentic self, and that is an ongoing process. And despite the negative experiences, I have had positive influences and experiences with brogrammers and things that I have learned that I feel like I should pass on.

I. Brogrammers Come in Variety Packs

Every time I would enter a new male-dominated team, I would immediately write them off as brogrammers. The reality was that I was over generalizing and not giving great team members a chance. I've learned that some of my best allies are straight men and I would have never learned that if I continued write them off as brogrammers.

Not all brogrammers are straight males, either. Hell, I was a walking testament to this. I am still a little bit of a brogrammer in recovery. Brogrammers come in all shapes and sizes but you can't just write people off or place a label because you might end up missing out on some really great folks.

2. Imposter Syndrome is Normal

If I could go back in time and tell junior-engineer-me one thing, it would be this: Imposter Syndrome is when you feel like you are pretending. It's when you feel like you are passing—when you feel like you don't know what the hell you are doing. When I first started as a systems admin, I had a permanent panic attack for months. All the guys I worked with were breezing through everything while I was still stuck on my first ticket. I was terrified that someone would find out that I had no idea what I was doing. It was worse when I would ask someone for help and he would come from across from the campus to solve my problem for me. For years, I thought I had this huge secret that I didn't know what I was doing because I kept asking for help and all of my brogrammer coworkers never asked for help. It wasn't until years later that I started having lunch with other women engineers did I find out that that is normal.

Most of the women I encounter constantly felt as though they were hiding that they didn't know what they were doing when in actuality, we were doing just fine. I had become my own worst critic, and I couldn't even see I was doing even better than some of my colleagues. I was feeling bad about my work, and didn't even appreciate that my builds always ran (while I can't say the same for the bros down the hall). Being constantly around competitive and boasting brogrammers will definitely make you question your confidence. You should remember that you've earned to be where you are. You have the skillset, the mindset and the only thing the brogrammers have over you is a surface level of confidence. We are just as good as they are, if not better. We're just less boastful about it.

3. Be the Driver

When you first start out as a junior engineer, I can guarantee you will be in a meeting with your product manager or your manager or (good luck) an end-user and you will hear requests that just sound impossible. They will ask you, we would like "Application A to talk to Application B using Communication C." Sounds simple, but as a junior engineer you hear, "We would like you to draw four red circles using these three green perpendicular lines." Needless to say, you will always come to a point where you should ask for help. The problem with asking a brogrammer for help is they will want keyboard control. Now to me, that tells me that they don't think I am capable or that they didn't find it worth the time to try and teach or show me how to do it.

When this happens you hold onto your keyboard, you don't git push or svn commit because what you will get in return is entirely rewritten code. You won't be learning anything or growing as a programmer. Instead, place value on learning that new skill. Don't ask if someone "has a minute," but rather schedule out time with that other person to sit and you figure it out together. This is not only the best way to learn but also a way to show that you're not a damsel in distress that needs saving.

4. High-Fives are Awesome

High-fives are like bro-juice. They love high-fives and I started to really love high-fives too. Bros high-five over everything. Finished a deploy? High-five. Fixed that bug? High-five! Got a beer from the fridge? Yeah! High-five. High-fiving was a way to congratulate and acknowledge each other on a job well done. This type of positive reinforcement helped me get over my imposter syndrome by making me feel like a valued team member. Instead of just being told what I did wrong, I was told what I did right and how I could improve. This also helped me give positive feedback to others and together our team fosters a culture of acknowledgement and constructive feedback.

5. Careers are not Ladders

This is my favorite. I know that "climbing up the corporate ladder" is a well-known saying, and that it reflects how we usually think of our careers. When I first got a job as software engineer, as a millennial, my first thought was "how do I become a senior engineer"? Did it matter that it was my first day as a software engineer? No. I just knew that was the next step and that is what I should work toward.

Brogrammers showed me that careers aren't always so linear. If they hit a wall with their career, if they feel unhappy or see money in another field, they will go there. This is how we ended up with brogrammers in the first place.

Careers are not ladders. It's rock climbing.

- It's hard
- It's not straight up
- You have to make your own path
- You have to have a great support system
- You have to trust yourself, there are a lot of risky moves
- You sometimes have to go a couple steps backwards in order to get a better route
- Sometimes you hit a plateau, but if you really want it, you will continue up

The point is that there is no one way up, but there is still a way to the top. You can get there.

THE PIPELINE ISN'T THE PROBLEM

Elissa Shevinsky

The Pipeline Problem: a narrative that states that the reason big tech companies have poor track records for hiring and promoting women is because there are too few women interested in or skilled in STEM (science, tech, engineering and math).

The idea that tech has a pipeline problem—one that can be solved by teaching five-year-old girls to code—infuriates me.

It's awkward to say so. I need to tread carefully here, lest I be accused of bad feminism. I can see the headline now: "#LADYBOSS Against STEM Education for Girls. Also Secretly Hates Puppies."

I am, of course, in favor of teaching girls to code. And it is true that there are more men than women applying for jobs and programs in Silicon Valley. But the reason why we don't have more women in tech is not because of a lack of STEM education. It's because too many high profile and influential individuals and sub-cultures within the tech industry have ignored or outright mistreated women applicants and employees. To be succinct—the problem isn't women, it's tech culture. That's the issue that needs to be addressed.

The mistake that we have made, as journalists and as readers, is taking the narratives espoused by executives at big tech companies at face value. Sometimes those executives, expressing deep concern about the "pipeline problem," are women. That doesn't mean that they are speaking as feminists. An executive woman at a company like Google or Yahoo is just as likely to be speaking on behalf her company—beholden to its quarterly revenue numbers and its many public shareholders.

We all know that there is a "Women in Tech" problem. But the nature of that problem looks very different, depending on your vantage point.

It's worth noting that sexism is not evenly distributed in Silicon Valley—or anywhere else that I have ever been. Some companies have healthy work environments and others do not. Companies like Google are quite large, and some departments are more dysfunctional than others. Moreover, things are far better for women in tech than they were even two or three years ago. It's not my aim to say that sexism is everywhere, or that we are all at fault. The work that I aim to do here is clarifying the nature of the "Women in Tech" problem, to the extent that we agree that something is wrong.

Note that the "pipeline problem" storyline is used not only about women but also about people of color, LGBTQ people, and pretty much any minority or group that doesn't have cultural fit.

The women who work in tech agree that the problem is harassment, discrimination and a generally hostile work environment. Many cite difficulties being hired, promoted, or getting funding. An overwhelming number of the highest profile technology companies have had a sexual harassment scandal that has made headlines—many within the last year. Whether its public companies like Google or Twitter or fast growing startups like Github, Uber, Snapchat, and Tinder, a job applicant would have good reasons to believe that she is about to join a fraternity. It is unsurprising that these companies have difficulty hiring women.

These are all variations of a problem where companies, and individual actors within companies, could do more to create professional and hospitable work environments. While cultural issues and HR practices are better or worse depending on the company or the team, there is a good deal of consensus among tech workers that this is the shape of the problem.

We should not look to executives at big companies to describe problems of sexism and inequality in

Silicon Valley. Executives at companies like Google or Yahoo have a different set of problems, and those are the issues that they will articulate when given a microphone. These issues include hiring the most talented people, while using the least amount of resources to do so. These problems include how best to create shareholder value, and how to do damage control around negative PR.

Putting the blame on the pipeline problem is good for PR and shareholder value because it shifts blame away from a tech company's leadership and HR departments, and onto women. This is a way for big tech companies to avoid hard conversations about fixing broken recruiting practices and fixing work environments that are hostile to women and people of color.

I understand this. As a CEO myself, I don't fault other executives for doing their jobs. I also optimize for shareholder valuation and reputation. However, I take their descriptions of tech problems with a grain of salt. When I see YouTube CEO Susan Wojcicki describing the pipeline problem, I see a representative of YouTube (which is owned by Google). Her problems are not the problems of most women in technology. Her problems are those of shareholders and board directors charged with optimizing quarterly revenues.

The "pipeline problem" narrative is a double win for big tech companies. It absolves them of responsibility for their faulty hiring practices and problematic work environments. It sweeps these issues under the rug.

The "pipeline problem" story also encourages the flow of resources toward training women and minorities to be knowledge workers. Increasing the pool of potential applicants is valuable for these companies. It is a way to hire more people without making any internal changes for recruitment. Efforts to improve the pipeline don't necessarily come with any obligations by these companies to hire or fairly treat these workers, once they are trained.

I worry about training and encouraging women to join an industry that is failing so many of the women who are already here.

Maximizing Google's shareholder value is fine (hey, making money is the American way) but it's not what's at stake when we talk about Silicon Valley's sexism problem. On reflection, turning to Google and Twitter executives to suggest solutions for sexism in tech is absurd. In the best cases they are describing someone else's problem. In some cases they are themselves the bad actors.

Equally troubling are the comments used to support the pipeline narrative. The subtext is that women currently aren't qualified to be hired or funded by Google, Twitter, or Y Combinator. This paints women as damsels in distress who need extra help to be part of Silicon Valley.

What makes me so certain about the issues facing women in tech? I've talked to hundreds of women in the course of writing essays for publications like *Business Insider*, and hosted "#LADYBOSS" parties for female founders. I also experienced many of these issues myself, consistently and repeatedly, during my first two years breaking into Silicon Valley culture.

I have been making software since 1997. That's a long time. I've been making GOOD software since 2004. That's over ten years and ten thousand woman hours— long enough to be a real expert, as defined by Malcolm Gladwell in his book "Outliers: The Story of Success." And I've been an expert software developer—good enough to run a software team—for about two years. At my last company, Glimpse, we delivered a new release on time and without major bugs, like clockwork, every month. I ran the tech team jointly with the CTO. He ran backend development, like devops and APIs. I focused on the front end development. I've played major roles on teams that built software used by millions of people, most notably SouthBeachDiet.com and dailysteals.com. DailySteals, at its peak, ranked #834 among the most highly-trafficked websites in the world.

I've also designed and led smaller teams, building products like Glimpse. Glimpse had five star ratings in the app store and 10–18 percent week-over-week traction. That's considered to be very good traction, by most Silicon Valley metrics.

My point is that I am more than qualified to be recruited by a big tech company (I've been qualified since 2001, when Massachusetts-based eZiba.com recruited me to join them as a Java developer.) But that hasn't been my experience.

In 2012 I was told by a senior manager at YouTube (a Google subsidiary) that I was not qualified for Google. I was told "Google only hires the best." Despite spending many days at YouTube and at Google, I was never recruited. I would go there to visit my housemate, my friends, or to meet with business contacts who worked at Google. I have eaten lunch at the YouTube HQ, Google Cambridge, and Google Mountain View. There was a time when I was a Google fangirl. I would have loved to have worked on Google+, back when that product was still promising.

I am known for having a lot of self-confidence. Claire Cain Miller, of the *New York Times*, described me as having "entrepreneurial brio." I do not have a confidence problem but I definitely integrated the idea that I would not be hired at Google.

In retrospect, I may have had opportunities if I had fought for them. But Google is espousing the idea that women are nowhere to be found. I was on campus, frequently, and would have been an easy recruit. Google can't ask for much more than for potential female hires to walk right onto campus, as I did frequently in 2011 and 2012.

I have brilliant female friends who have applied for roles at Google and other tech companies, and have also been rejected. I am very curious to understand why.

In 2014 and 2015, I applied to developer conferences at Facebook and Twitter. Just like Google, Facebook and Twitter's employees and leadership are mostly white and male. And just like Google, those companies justify their demographics by citing a lack of women and minority applicants.

My team had integrated Facebook and Twitter's developer tools (APIs) in innovative ways, as part of our efforts to protect user privacy. I could answer any question about their APIs. So you would think that I was an ideal candidate for their developer conferences. So far I have shipped three different products using Facebook's API. Despite this, I have consistently been rejected from Facebook and Twitter's developer conferences—even as they claim that they cannot find enough women to hire and promote.

So when I hear these companies say that they cannot find women, I am confused. I'm here. My friends are here. We are even knocking on their doors. We are applying to their conferences and for jobs and internships and funding. We are signing into their headquarters as guests and using their APIs. We are easy to find on LinkedIn and through our social networks. And with well over ten thousand (wo)man hours spent building web applications used by millions of people, I am comfortable saying that I'm qualified. My friends are qualified too.

So let's stop saying that women aren't here, or that they aren't skilled. Let's instead look at why we're not seeing/hiring/promoting/funding/respecting the women who are.

As Aliya Rahman tweeted at the Lesbians Who tech conference, "I believe the best way to hire women and people of colors is to hire them."

Sometimes I think it really is that simple. The best way to hire more women is to hire them. We are already here, and we are already awesome.

*

Things were different when I got started in tech.

When I got into programming as a teenager, I felt very welcome in Computer Science. It was 1997, and I was taking CSCI 105: "The Web: Technologies and Techniques," the Computer Science department's most introductory class. It seemed like a lightweight way for a humanities major like me to fulfill the college's science requirement. I had just graduated from a science high school, and wanted to take a break from challenging STEM classes. This seemed perfect.

Led by Professor Tom Murtagh, the class covered the architecture of the Internet, along with html and Java programming. My teaching assistants were nerdy white guys (who I totally admired) but the class was mostly gender balanced. In 1997 we didn't know that programming was for boys.

Computer Science 105 was more challenging than I had anticipated. It was hard enough to get the code for my Java applet to run. It was even harder for me to make sense of the various file systems and directories; the notion of uploading a file to the Internet was an entirely new concept. I was so frustrated that a program could work on my machine and not work correctly on my website. At one point the teaching assistant was confused as well! I've since learned that frustration is a basic part of software development. The best developers are persistent as well as smart, and simply don't stop until the code works. Sometimes it takes days or weeks. At the time, I just thought that I didn't have an aptitude for programming. But Professor Murtagh (aka "Tom") was a warm and easy-going professor, and the class was incredibly fun.

We took a class trip to wire up ethernet cables, so the local elementary school would have Internet. I remember working with Tom and my classmates, following instructions for installing yellow and red wires. It was all so friendly. I remember liking my political science class more, but feeling like Computer Science was there, as a warm and welcoming option, if I ever decided it was interesting or relevant. Remarkably, I felt this way despite also believing that I was not very good at Computer Science.

The industry was so new. We didn't have role models like Zuck or Jobs to create "pattern recognition" for hiring managers or Venture Capitalists. Zuck hadn't even begun high school in 1997. Jobs had not yet turned Apple into the iconic company it would eventually become. In 1997, before the iPod and iPhone and Macbook Pro, Apple was described as a "damaged brand." (http://allaboutstevejobs.com/bio/timeline.php)

We didn't have ten years of white male heroes. We had each other. Nerds against the world!

In 1997, this was a battle that us nerds had not yet won. Nerds were so uncool at Williams College that the section of campus where we lived was known as "The Odd Quad." There were no hackathons or multi-million dollar acquisitions by Facebook. It was just a bunch of us in the "Sun Lab" talking about TCP protocol and making websites that no one saw. The programmer-nerds became my friends. We would get together on Wednesday nights for hot cocoa spiked with liquor, and play "Magic: The Gathering."

It was a gender balanced group. Actually, it was nearly equally men and women. They were all paired up, in these heterosexual couples of male and female programmers. I was paired up too; my boyfriend taught me to write Perl code and pick locks. My college memories are mostly of hanging out with this group of wonderful nerdy gamer coders. This included some college grads who were working at Tripod, a local tech startup. Tripod sold to Lycos for $58M in stock. That success led to the creation of the Village Ventures VC fund, which supported the development of dozens of other tech companies in Williamstown and nearby North Adams.

Some of my alumni friends had gone on to work at those other startups. I would visit them, taking naps on the company couch and drinking beer on Friday afternoons. I have the fondest early memories of tech culture.

I got internship and job offers everywhere that I applied, ultimately working for Ethan Zuckerman's startup Geekcorps. We sent tech geeks to Ghana. I remember being offered a programming job at twenty-one. I would have had to drop out of school, which wasn't that interesting to me at the time. I turned the job down. But I always felt like technology—computer science—wanted me. I had friends in the industry, I had job offers, I fit into that world. That's a powerful thing, to feel wanted. Like you belong. Like you know what to do. Like you're among friends. Safe. Respected.

Fast forward to now.

Put yourself in the shoes of a young woman considering career choices, and doing initial research. If she were to research working at a large tech company, what would she find? And if she were to apply, what would she experience?

It's time that we stopped saying that women aren't interested in tech or in programming or in STEM, and that special education for women is the solution. Women were interested in tech when I was coming of age, and it was a decent place to be. Smart applicants do research before they enter a new field. And it doesn't take much research to realize that technology has a gender problem. Smart women are making a well-educated decision when they choose a non-STEM field.

Upon close examination, a woman researching tech might realize that there are amazing opportunities for those who are willing to navigate the landscape. But not every applicant will get past the initial hesitation, and many do not have mentors or role models to help them find that awesome first job or angel investor.

It's with this in mind that I encourage women to get involved in tech, but to do so by working closely with a trusted mentor. Startups like Glassbreakers offer peer-to-peer mentoring for women in tech. There are definitely paths for women to have awesome experiences developing their skills and becoming successful in technology. But those paths take some work to find. Other industries may seem easier or less risky. Any candidate that is smart and savvy enough to do well in tech could become successful in any number of other fields.

As a teenager and young adult, I turned down many lucrative opportunities (management consulting was all the rage in 1999) when I chose to work with my friends at tech startups. I might not have made that choice if my research had suggested that the tech industry had problems, or if my initial experiences with tech culture had been off-putting. I definitely got into tech because my friends were here, and they loved it.

So the issue is not that women need better or different education. The issue is what women find when they research our industry, and what their opportunities and experiences look like once they are here.

If we want top candidates to join us in technology, then we need to earn them.

Let's start by no longer perpetuating the following wrong and harmful narratives:

- that the reason there aren't more women working at big tech companies is because there simply aren't enough talented, interested, skilled women

- that improving STEM education is the magic bullet to fixing technology's gender imbalance
- that women need special education in order to participate in the tech economy
- that tech companies can improve recruitment without making significant internal changes

Let's stop blaming women for the failure of big tech companies and VCs to appreciate, respect, hire, fund, and promote them. And let's stop trying to solve an urgent, time-sensitive HR problem—the need for big companies to create genuinely hospitable environments for a diverse set of employees—with unrelated measures like teaching kindergarteners how to code or feel-good conferences that don't change how women are hired, promoted, funded or respected.

Women are not the problem. Let's fix the thing that is.

BUILD A BUSINESS, NOT AN EXIT STRATEGY

Melanie Moore

Melanie Moore is my Lean Out *hero. She is building a real business, on her own terms. And the best part? This could be me, or you. Melanie is living a dream that is real, and attainable. And her advice? "Follow your own path." This essay is the antidote to drinking the start-up Kool-Aid, and was originally a talk she gave at PulsoConf in Bogota in September 2012.*

How many people reading this have a startup? How many people reading this are trying to raise capital for that startup?

Let me just lay out the odds for you. Only 1 percent of all companies will ever raise VC. And, of those who do raise institutional capital, only 2 percent of those companies will have an exit north of $100 million. And if that exit does come, the founders will own, most likely, one-third or less of their own company by that time. Because, by the time you get to an exit of that size, the founders have been diluted down by three or four rounds of capital. This means that the founders have a 0.02 percent chance of personally taking home $30 million. And if you have co-founders? Divide that number by two or three. Now, you may be saying, "But $30 million is a lot of money" or, "Hell, $15 million is a lot of money." But that is not the way you should evaluate the risk / reward proposition in this scenario. You have to look at the expected value of that $15 million.

For the uninitiated, expected value is the probability of an event, expressed as a dollar amount. For example, if you have a choice between a 5 percent chance of winning $1,000 or a 20 percent chance of winning $300, statistically, you should choose the latter, as that has an expected value of $60, while the first scenario has an expected value of $50.

So, let's do the math: multiply $100,000,000 by 1 percent, which is the chance you have of raising VC, then by 2 percent, which is the chance of $100 million+ exit, then by 33 percent, which is the average amount of the company that the founders will still own after said exit, and then again by 50 percent, assuming there are two founders. That is an expected value of $3,300. Three grand.

Now, let's say you start a small web-based SaaS business that solves a real problem for some segment of your market. Let's say you help entrepreneurs with their taxes at a lower cost than an accountant would charge.

Let's say you work on this start-up for ten years, and it becomes profitable after two years on revenue of $1 million per year. Let's say you have a profit margin of 20 percent, and you exit the business after ten years for $2 million, or 2x revenue. You never take money, and you are the only founder. Maybe you give away a small amount of equity to your first employees, but you still own 90 percent of the business.

Still difficult to do, but certainly not impossible. Now, the survival rate for small businesses, according to the United States Small Business Administration is 44 percent. I know, that sounds really surprising, as many of us are used to hearing that 95 percent or 99 percent of all businesses fail. But, in reality, only about 56 percent of small businesses fail in the first five years. Now, not all of those businesses make $1 million or more each year in revenue; only about the top 25 percent of small businesses make more than $1 million per year.

Let's do the math on this one, shall we? Ok, so add up your exit value of $2 million plus $1,600,000 in profit that you have paid out to yourself. That is $3.6 million, now multiply that times the small business survival rate of 44 percent, then again by 90 percent, which, in this scenario, is how much of the company you still own at exit. That is an expected value of $356,400. That is over 100x greater than the expected value of a VC-backed, high-growth tech startup. Granted, $3.6 million is not "fuck you" money, but it is certainly more money than I have ever seen.

Now, assuming you have bought into my argument thus far, let's look at exactly what it might take to build this mythical $1 million run-rate, profitable, web-based business.

There are actually only two steps you need to take to build this business. First, you need to build a product that at least some small segment of the market wants. Ok, that is easier said than done, but if you focus on a sufficiently niche segment, especially if it is in an industry or space that you know well, you are likely to be able to find a problem that you can solve that no one else is solving in quite the way you are. Now, this does not need to be the most amazing business idea ever created, it does not even need to be all that revolutionary, it just needs to solve a problem for some people. How many people for which this product needs to solve a problem depends entirely on the second step.

Now, listen carefully, because this is really important. It may seem a little crazy, but trust me, this is the key to building a successful business: you have to actually SELL your product, you know, for money. Now, how much money? Well, that depends on what you are selling. Are you selling B2B SaaS solution that helps small businesses manage their taxes? Then maybe you charge $30 a month. Or are you selling a luxury consumer product, that only a few people want or can afford? Then maybe you charge thousands of dollars. Either way, the math is simple: number of purchases x price of each unit sold = revenue.

Let's say you have a web-based business that helps small businesses manage their taxes and you charge $30 / month. That means you only need about 2,800 customers to make $1 million each year in revenue. That's it, 2,800 people. And to do this in two years? That means you only have to add three or four customers each DAY! Four people a day. You could do that by just cold calling your existing customers and giving them six months free if they get 1 friend to sign-up.

Now, I don't want to make it seem like building a sustainable, profitable business with millions in revenue is easy, but it is certainly a lot easier than most other founders and VCs would have you believe. And that is because, for founders trying to build billion dollar companies and VCs chasing the next Instagram mirage, it IS really, really, really hard to build a business to that size and growth rate. It is 0.02 percent hard.

But, if it's THAT hard, why do founders and VCs keep going after these types of "go big or go home" investments? In order to understand why, you have to understand the incentive structure of venture capital firms. VC firms are just like any other institutional investor like a private equity or hedge fund. They have LPs, or Limited Partners, which are usually big insurance companies, pension funds, or university endowments that have billions upon billions of dollars that they must hold for decades. Usually, these LPs allocate some small percent of those funds toward "alternative investments" like venture capital. LPs decide how much and to whom money is allocated. LPs decide whether the Partners at a particular fund get to keep their jobs, and they base these decisions on one thing: returns. Ideally, extraordinarily high returns. These funds all have, basically, the same mandate. They raise a fund, maybe $100 million, and then they will have ten years to invest, exit, and return the fund. The mandate is to return 3x or more to their LPs within ten years. This creates some very interesting, and perverse, incentive structures.

First, in order to exit all or most of the fund's investments within ten years, the majority of this money must be invested, or earmarked for future investment in existing portfolio companies, within the first four years of the fund. Most funds only write ten to twelve checks a year. And, with a fund size of $100 million, the partners cannot, logistically, invest in small, profitable, steadily growing businesses, because they would have to invest in hundreds of them in order to put all of that capital to work. It is just not logistically feasible for only four to eight partners to do this within the first four years of a fund.

Second, LPs expect at least a 3x return on the entire fund at the end of the ten-year mandate. Now, consider that, on average, 80 percent of a fund's investments will fail. Another 15 percent will return 2x or 3x. And the top 5 percent of the fund's investments will return 10x or more. The fund will continue to invest larger sums in its most successful investments as those businesses grow, while the ones that do not meet expectations will not receive additional funding, and thus, will have lost a smaller percentage of money for the fund than the big wins will have gained. Even accounting for this, most funds will return far less than 3x, most will fail. The only way to win is to be an early investor in the biggest wins, which, even if all of the fund's other investments fail, will make up for all of those losses, and return the entire fund.

Once you understand this, you begin to understand why VCs hammer home the "pick a big market" and "network effects" mantras, because that is the only way they make money! I'm not saying VCs are bad people or are looking to manipulate you. I'm just saying that VCs are doing the absolute most rational thing they can: they are responding to their own incentive structure; it is human nature. But that does not mean taking VC is the best possible decision for you, or the only way to build a big or successful business. Quite the opposite.

You need to think about the lifestyle you want, and the goals that are important to you. People in this industry act like if you are not working eighty hours a week and sleeping under your desk, somehow you are failing, or you are "not meant to be an entrepreneur." Well, I am here to tell you that that is absolute bullshit. Look, if you are so extraordinarily passionate about what you are working on that you can't wait to hop out of bed at 6 a.m. and head to the office for a fourteen-hour day, by all means, knock yourself out. But don't do it because you think that is what you are "supposed" to do. Don't think that, just because you have passions and goals outside of your startup, that somehow you aren't committed enough or you aren't going to succeed. I find that if you can just focus for a full four or five hours a day, uninterrupted, on your startup, that that is enough. Maybe when you have a release coming up, you have to put in more hours, but there is no way to be really productive for fourteen straight hours a day, at least not consistently.

A little anecdote: I have a friend of mine who runs a relatively well-known startup in NYC. He literally LIVES at the office. I'm serious, he moved in. And before that, he slept on the couch most nights. And, after working this hard for almost two years, guess how much revenue this startup is generating? Zero. Not a fucking penny. After two years of work! Now, I understand that they are trying to build a massive user base with network effects, blah blah blah, but, I'm sorry, that is absolutely fucking insane. I could never see myself living my life that way. I am just not built for it. To put in that many years of your life, and thousands of hours of work, for what will most likely turn out to be an unsuccessful startup, is just crazy to me. But, from reading the tech press, you would think this is one of the hottest startups in New York!

Which brings me to my next point: don't drink the tech Kool-Aid, it's not good for you. And frankly, it's not even that tasty. When all you read about is funding after funding after funding, you begin to believe that that is the only way to be a successful startup. How many times have you read a story about a startup that took no funding, has only one founder, worked quietly for two or three years, and is now generating over $2 million in revenue? I'm guessing never. That's not interesting, I suppose. That story doesn't sell papers. But you know what? Those are the truly successful entrepreneurs, the ones who spent years building a profitable, sustainable business, with not a lot of outside help and very little start-up capital. People like the founder of Subway, who still owns 100 percent of the company, which is now the largest franchise in the world, or Sara Blakely, who turned $5,000 and a pair of footless pantyhose into a billion dollar business called Spanx. Those are the people we should be talking about, celebrating, and looking up to.

Unfortunately, I had to learn all of this the hard way. In 2009, fresh off of a stint as an investment banker, I started my first company, called ToVieFor, which was in the apparel space, and also happened to be a total fucking disaster.

I think I was stuck in my career, and was really just more excited by the idea of running a tech startup rather than building a real business. And we did well for a while. We won the NYU Business Plan Competition and received a $75,000 grant from NYU, we were one out of only twenty-five companies invited to launch, on stage, at TechCrunch Disrupt in San Francisco, and then, most impressive of all, we were selected as one out of eleven startups to be a part of the inaugural class of the TechStars accelerator program in New York City. Almost 1,000 companies applied, only the top 1 percent were chosen. I still consider this to be one of my greatest professional accomplishments.

And TechStars is really an amazing program. You meet people you would never otherwise meet, you have access to some of the top investors in the world, and you make lifelong friends with the other founders. But TechStars stays true to its promise of being an accelerator. It accelerates your company in exactly the direction you were already heading. Have a little bit of tension among the founding team? Expect for at least one founder break-up during the program. Putting a ton of money into acquiring users with little success? Expect to get absolutely grilled by every investor you meet and have your competency questioned. Hired an engineer that is not totally committed? Expect her to leave when things get tough. TechStars, like many accelerators, accelerates both the good and the bad. It, like VC funding, is rocket fuel, and if you are not ready, your company will explode upon impact.

And that is exactly what happened to us. A spectacular explosion that included: a very public founder break-up, horrible gossip pieces in the press, and a reality TV show to document it all. Lovely.

So, my choice at that point was either: head back into the safe, warm arms of Corporate America or, take the lessons I learned and use them to build a real business. You can guess that I choose the latter.

I started my latest company, Elizabeth & Clarke, by myself, bringing on a part-time technical co-founder several months in to help build the first product. With only $75 dollars in start-up capital, and one month spent building a minimum viable product together, we began to generate revenue. Now, one year in, we just hit profitability. I estimate that I sunk in an additional $5,000 of personal savings this past year. But that's it, I own 95 percent of the business, have never taken money, and we are profitable and growing at 20 percent a month.

So, at the end of the day, what does all this mean for you? First, you can do the same thing I did, you can build a profitable, small web-based business in just a few years, take a great salary and work thirty hours per week. But more than that, my message is not, "do as I do," it's "follow your own path." Don't listen to investors or the press or even me. Take advice, sure, but do what you really want to do, and don't feel bad about it because somebody else may not call it "success." Second, solve your own problem. No matter what path you take as an entrepreneur, small business or large, this is really the best way to find success. And, whatever you do, DO NOT drink the Kool-Aid! You can trust me on that one.

WHERE DO WE GO FROM HERE?

Lauren Bacon

Today's feminism feels dispersed. A lawsuit here, a tweetstorm there, someone gets fired. Are we making progress? How would we know? One set of feminists achieves a goal, and another group writes posts about how that effort was counter-productive. It sometimes feels as if different feminists are working at cross purposes, because often, in fact, we are. And yet, there are a number of social changes that we could all get behind.

Lauren Bacon's essay poses essential questions: What are our collective goals, and how will we get there? What if we worked together?

2014 was a harrowing year for women in the tech world. Google (followed quickly by other Silicon Valley heavy-hitters) released its diversity data, and the numbers were as disappointing as we expected).[1] Tinder co-founder and former VP Marketing Whitney Wolfe filed a sexual harassment and sex-based discrimination lawsuit against the company.[2] Tech conferences, from OSCON to DEFCON, continued to come under scrutiny for failing to protect women attendees' safety. Game developers Zoe Quinn and Brianna Wu received rape and death threats, and video game critic Anita Sarkeesian was forced to cancel a speech at Utah State University after receiving death threats and threats to attendees. And Kathy Sierra, an influential thinker who famously left the spotlight in 2007 after being subjected to horrific online abuse, shut down her Twitter account, saying, "Life for women in tech, today, is often better the less visible they are."[3]

It was also the year that people in my life who don't work in tech seemed to become aware that the tech

---

[1] "You Call This Diversity? A Disappointing Snapshot of Silicon Valley," by Kimberly Weisul. Inc., June 18, 2014. http://www.inc.com/kimberly-weisul/you-call-this-diversity-new-data-from-silicon-valley.html

[2] "Tinder Is Target of Sexual Harassment Lawsuit," by Jenna Wortham. The New York Times, July 1, 2014. http://www.nytimes.com/2014/07/02/business/media/tinder-is-target-of-sexual-harassment-lawsuit.html

[3] Kathy Sierra, "Trouble at the Kool-Aid Point," October 7, 2014. http://seriouspony.com/trouble-at-the-koolaid-point/

industry has a serious problem with women. Gamergate got so huge and nasty that it was widely reported—and with so many people playing video games these days, it looked to me, for a moment, like we might have reached a tipping point for public awareness. Friends who play games, but don't design them—who use technology, but don't build it—were posting articles about Gamergate on social media.

Then, of course, the story receded from the news cycle, as these things do. And I was left wondering: Where do we go from here?

Because after getting a glimpse into a world where gender discrimination in tech is on everyone's radar, and where online harassment is deemed unacceptable, it's clear to me that it's actually possible to make these concerns a majority issue. We have more allies than I used to believe we did.

We just need to cultivate them—and build a movement.

Which brings me to a rather big question.

Are feminists in tech willing to embrace the idea that we are building a social movement?

Some days, when the hashtags are flying and the calls to action are clear, I feel optimistic that we are. Other days, when yet another *Lean In*-inspired flamewar erupts, the answer seems less obvious.

It makes sense that we might resist such a label. Techies are a notoriously label-averse group, for starters—and even the most socially conscious among us lean, as a group, toward individualism over anything that might smack of orthodoxy.

But the range and scale of change for which we are advocating are significant enough that I would argue we are part of a social movement, whether we like it or not. The good news here is that there is a huge body of work available to us for considering how to build and expand such a movement, and how to drive forward an agenda for change.

I am no visionary; I don't have a grand plan for tech feminism's future. But I do have some thoughts on the immediate, practical questions we need to address if we techie feminists were to agree to band together under the "social movement" umbrella and plot a course for the future we want to see. Until we answer these questions, individually and collectively, we risk getting stuck with the status quo.

Perhaps the most critical question we must consider is a fundamental one: what is our collective goal?

Is it simply to get more women into tech? Most of us seem to agree that's a goal worth pursuing, although even here, I hear some disagreement—for instance, should we be focusing on getting more women into technical roles? Into leadership positions? Or simply relying on critical mass to tip the scales? Is it to fight the great feminist fight within the context of our workplaces, exposing and addressing gender bias and injustice wherever we find it? Are we content to make inroads into the existing system (by which I mean the dominant paradigm that's touted in

Silicon Valley and beyond, a VC-fuelled hypercapitalist meritocracy)—or do we want to totally dismantle the master's house and build something new in its place? These are massive questions, and we don't need to reach agreement on them. But we do owe it to each other to acknowledge that many of us will answer them differently—and that so long as we can agree on a handful of strategic goals, there is power in working together to achieve them.

This is the lesson handed down by every successful social movement in recent history: strategic alliances, focused relentlessly on their common goals, get results. These alliances may be tense, and they are likely to be temporary, but they're among the most effective tools available to us.

To cite just one recent example, when the state of New York legalized marriage equality in 2011, it was the culmination of a calculated, concerted effort on the part of four groups that had not always worked well together: the Empire State Pride Agenda, the Human Rights Campaign, Freedom to Marry, and Marriage Equality New York. Two years prior, the groups had campaigned hard for similar legislation, but failed due to conflicting messages and approaches. To win in 2011, they had to set aside differences and agree on a single common strategy.[4]

---

[4] "Cuomo Helps Groups Mobilize for Gay Marriage Bill," by Michael Barbaro. The New York Times, April 19, 2011. http://www.nytimes.com/2011/04/20/nyregion/cuomo-helping-rights-groups-on-gay-marriage-effort.html

If feminists in tech can agree that our odds of making inroads toward positive change are better when we work together, perhaps we can look at a few leverage points—and specific strategic goals—where alliances can be built to strengthen our likelihood of success.

A Necessary Caveat

It's been my experience that movements working toward diversity are necessarily fragmented and, well, diverse. I'm a big believer that we don't all have to think the same way, or want the same things, in order to collaborate effectively.

I'm also not suggesting that alliances are for everyone. The lion may not lie down with the lamb for long, and neither are the Sandberg diehards likely to become BFFs with more radical, overthrow-the-system types. But the history of social movements tells us that some pretty uncomfortable alliances have been formed in times of need.

While I'm in no way suggesting that we all disregard (or deny) our differences in favor of some utopian confederation of techie feminists, I would argue that building targeted—and temporary—strategic alliances is one of the best ways we can move toward effecting real change.

Where are the Leverage Points?

Perhaps the first step in forging alliances is defining the opportunities where working together can net real results—and that means defining our common goals.

Some of the clear possibilities I see for alliance-building are:

- *Addressing online harassment:* making it safer for women to participate in online spaces without fear of threats, harassment, and/or doxxing.
- *Increased participation:* defining barriers to women entering, and participating in, the tech world—and advancing solutions to these issues.
- *Moving women into leadership:* establishing strategic goals that support women in tech to advance their careers, and encourage tech companies to address gender disparity in the C-suite and boardroom.
- *Reducing attrition:* identifying factors that drive women to drop out of tech at double the rate of men, and proposing solutions.
- *Increasing access to funding for women entrepreneurs:* addressing the massive disparity in access to financing (both from banks and investors) that women face compared to men.
- *Creating alternate models of support for women entrepreneurs:* for those who prefer to bootstrap, or pursue forms of investment other than venture capital, developing prototypes and documenting successes and failures.

None of these ideas are new; in fact, all of these strategies are well-established and in use by various groups working toward gender diversity in tech. My point is not to invent new goals, but rather to identify those that seem most likely to appeal to a broad support base within the movement and provide fertile ground for alliances.

It's also worth noting here that each of the above bullet points contains ample opportunity for forming alliances beyond tech feminism. Issues of harassment, participation, leadership, attrition, access to funding and entrepreneurial support systems affect not only women, but people of color, transgender people, people with disabilities, and other structurally marginalized groups. And there are tons of folks in the tech world who are exploring alternatives to what Maciej Ceglowski calls the "investor storytime" model. So we would do well to cast our net wide when looking for potential allies.

And we can do that by asking ourselves, once we commit ourselves to a particular goal, "Who else would consider this a win?"

A MAP for Building a Movement

Social justice activist Bill Moyer published a fascinating, in-depth analysis of social movements in 1987 called The Movement Action Plan, in which he describes an 8-stage arc that successful social movements follow.[5] According to Moyer, the stages are as follows:

- Critical social problem exists (business as usual)
- Prove failure of official institutions (normal channels fail)

---

[5] http://www.historyisaweapon.com/defcon1/moyermap.html

- Ripening conditions (growing discontent and an emerging opposition movement; can take years to develop) [Trigger event: a highly publicized, shocking event that makes the public take notice]
- Take off (everyone is talking about this social problem)
- Perception of failure (general population divided about 50/50; activists lose faith and experience burnout)
- Majority public opinion (eroding supports for power holders)
- Success (social consensus emerges in support of the movement's proposed alternatives)
- Continuation (moving on)

I would argue that tech feminism is still in Stage 2 (or perhaps 3); we are still in the process of documenting and proving that the existing institutions and infrastructure aren't working, although public awareness is certainly on the rise.

Looking at the movement through this lens helps me realize a few things:

- We ought to pace ourselves. Activists are well-advised to practice self-care along the way, because we are running a marathon here, not a sprint.
- Now is a great time to run experiments. We are still in startup mode. The timing is perfect for designing lean startup-style hypotheses to test out, while the

    stakes are still relatively low and we have lots of learning to do.

- While it's tempting to focus on what Moyer calls "the powerholders" (those in charge of institutions, money and other influential resources), those people will likely not budge unless public opinion shifts first; they are too invested in the status quo. Put another way, until the majority of people consider it unacceptable that women face massive discrimination in the tech world, the powerholders will not change. So our focus should be on influencing public opinion.

To elaborate on that last point: the core principle of Moyer's MAP is that the goal of every social movement is to win over the hearts and minds of the majority of the population—and the central strategy for doing this is to appeal to widely-held values of justice, freedom, democracy and human rights, and demonstrate that the status quo (as upheld by the powerholders) violates these principles.

    In the case of gender inequality within the technology industry, we still have a long way to go to convince the majority of the population that inequality is a systemic issue; but if we are to do so, the most compelling argument we may be able to make centers around the discrepancy between the tech industry's view of itself as a gender- and color-blind meritocracy, and the reality that women comprise somewhere between 12-20 percent of technical positions, 26 percent of leadership positions, and 26 percent of the overall computing workforce (with African-Americans and Latinos/Latinas also significantly underrepresented compared to their numbers in the American workforce writ large). And just 7 percent of venture capital funding goes to women-owned businesses, despite the fact that startups with women executives are more than twice as likely to succeed.

These are not the kinds of figures we should expect from a true meritocracy. For a culture that prides itself on being a level playing field, it's clear that the field could be more aptly described as sloped, pitted, and laced with sand traps. Online harassment is another wedge issue that could provide huge leverage. The frequency and intensity of harassment that women experience online is so severe—and legal recourses are so limited—that odds are good that everyone knows at least one woman who has been harassed online.[6]

We've seen with Gamergate that popular sympathy lies with the victims of harassment, so ongoing efforts to raise awareness and pursue solutions—such as the legal reforms proposed by law professor Danielle Keats Citron[7]—seem likely to succeed so long as we are consistent about moving them forward.

---

[6] "Online Harassment: Summary of Findings," by Maeve Duggan. Pew Research, October 22, 2014. http://www.pewinternet.org/2014/10/22/online-harassment/

[7] Hate Crimes in Cyberspace, Danielle Keats Citron. Harvard University Press, 2014.

If techie feminists are willing to embrace being part of a social movement, then our immediate task is to address a few key questions:

- What is our collective goal?
- What specific leverage points should we focus on? (And more specifically, which ones have the greatest influence on public opinion?)
- Where are there opportunities for alliance building? (Or, "Who else would consider this a win?")
- What experiments can we design to test out potential solutions? (And how can we share our learning with one another so that successful experiments can be repeated?)
- How can we practice personal self-care to prevent burnout and support sustainable, long-term engagement with these issues?

I would love to see each of us engaging with these questions—on our blogs, at conferences, within existing groups that are working on gender equity in the tech world—so that as we work toward our individual goals and priorities, we also contribute to a bigger conversation about where we are going.

If we want to reach the momentum needed for large-scale change, we must learn from the change-makers who have come before us, and apply the lessons they learned.

YOU MUST START UP
FAKEGRIMLOCK

ME, FAKEGRIMLOCK, ONLY ROBOT STARTUP DINOSAUR
YOU GOING TO READ IN THIS BOOK, TELL YOU
SOMETHING.

YOU MUST STARTUP.
LOOK AROUND. THIS NOT WHAT WORLD COULD BE.
THIS NOT WHAT WORLD
SHOULD BE. THIS NOT WHAT WORLD MUST BE.
YOU WILL FIX IT.

YOU WILL NEED SKILLS. GET THEM. LEARN TO CODE.
LEARN TO UX. LEARN TO BUSINESS. YOU HAVE
COMPUTER AND INTERNET. IT FULL OF LEARN FOR
FREE. PRICE IS SWEAT AND PAIN. DO IT.
YOU WILL NEED COFOUNDERS. FIND THEM. GO TO
WHERE PEOPLE BURN. FIND CLASSES. EVENTS.
HACKATHONS. MOVE TO NEW CITY. KICK DOWN DOORS.

DO WHATEVER IT TAKE TO MEET PEOPLE WITH SKILLS.
PEOPLE READY TO CHANGE THE WORLD. PEOPLE LIKE
YOU.

YOU WILL NEED IDEA. MAKE ONE. WORLD FULL OF
THINGS YOU "CAN'T." FIND ONE YOU BURN TO "CAN."
MAKE FIST OF CODE. PUNCH TINY "CAN" INTO THE
WORLD. KEEP PUNCHING UNTIL IT HUGE.

YOU WILL NEED MONEY. EARN IT. TEAM WITH SKILLS
BUILD IDEA TO CHANGE WORLD. ONCE WORLD BEGIN
TO CHANGE, MONEY WILL FIND YOU. PUNCH UNTIL
THAT HAPPEN.

YOU WILL FAIL. OWN IT. OTHER PEOPLE FAIL, CRY, AND
GIVE UP. YOU ARE NOT OTHER PEOPLE.

YOU WILL GET BACK UP. YOU WILL PUNCH THE WORLD.
AGAIN AND AGAIN AND AGAIN.

WITH BETTER SKILLS. BETTER IDEA. BETTER
EVERYTHING. YOU WILL FAIL AND GET UP AND PUNCH
THE WORLD UNTIL IT CRACK IN HALF WITH "CAN" BIG
ENOUGH FOR EVERYONE.
YOU WILL STARTUP.
IT WILL BE HARD. IT WILL BE AMAZING. IT ONLY FOR
MOST DRIVEN, MOST TALENTED, MOST CREATIVE PEOPLE.

MAKE YOU ONE OF THEM.

ACKNOWLEDGEMENTS

This book owes so much to each of its authors. I am grateful for their willingness to share their stories, especially given the risks that accompany being outspoken on gender issues. The most prominent feminists receive death and rape threats on a regular basis. This book would not be possible if it were not for the willingness of my collaborators to put much needed social change ahead of their personal comfort. It is such an honor to publish their stories.

I am grateful, always, to my family. Mom and Dad, thank you. How many pages would it be if I listed all the ways that you've supported and encouraged me? Mom, thank you for the pride in your voice when you talk about the time that I wrote a small book, as a small child.

As I edited this collection, I thought about the influences that make me willing to be the only woman in the room. I owe that to my mom. My mother is fierce, brilliant, creative, an individualist. She was one of the top American painters in the late sixties. She was a woman painter in a field dominated by men. She signed her work "H. Shevinsky" so that her work would not be gendered. She taught me to never let anything hold me back or keep me down.

My grandmother was also strong. I remember as a small child being told that if a burglar broke into the house, it would be ok—because my nana would hit him over the head with a frying pan. I grew up thinking that was how all homes were protected, by an army of grandmas with frying pans. My grandfather was, in contrast, gentle and generous. He paid for my first writing class, as a high school student, at Cornell University.

The women in my family were so strong that I also grew up believing that the world was some kind of matriarchy. I remember the moment when my mom told me that there were people in the world who favored boys. I did not believe her. I had never been made to feel like I was less because I was a girl, at least not with my family. It was my dad who first suggested that sexism was the reason why I was not promoted faster at Everyday Health.

My dad taught me much needed Zen-discipline. I relied on him and my mom a good deal over the last few years. Entrepreneurship has been, at times, cold, lonely, difficult. Friends and cofounders have come and gone. My parents have always been there.

When I think back to being young, I remember boys (and some grown-up men) as bullies. I can understand why some women give in to the misandry. Real misandry, the kind that is not ironic. I have been there. It was the kindness and good natures of my dad and my grandfather that showed me that men could be a different way. It's because of them that I can see men as potential partners, allies, collaborators.

I remember the first time that I met Justin Humphries. I had wandered up to the OR Books table at the HopeX (Hackers of Planet Earth) conference and introduced myself. Justin had already read my essay "That's It, I'm Finished Defending Sexism in Tech." Always the salesman, I pitched him my book idea within minutes. But it was Justin who ultimately sold me on building this book right away, and doing it with OR Books. That happened because it was easy to believe in him as a creative partner and collaborator.

This was my first book, and Justin coached me through each step. He taught me what makes for a good anthology, and helped reach out to potential contributors. It was Justin's influence that helped make this book raw, authentic, meaningful. I could easily have written a generic book on leadership. I'm glad that I didn't.

Good collaborators are a rare and wonderful thing, and that is how I think of Justin.

OR Books co-founder John Oakes and the rest of the OR Books team have each been such a pleasure to work with that it merits naming each of them. John, thank you for your personal attention to *Lean Out*, and for what you have created at OR Books. We have gotten this far in our collaboration, and I remain enamored of you, your entire team and the OR Books vision. Here's to the future of publishing!

Courtney Andujar designed the cover. I love it and I think it's perfect. I am just getting started with Matthew Schantz and Emily Freyer on publicity and outreach. Already having fun—Matt and Emily, thank you in advance. See ya on Twitter!

Pax Dickinson introduced me to the folks at *Business Insider*. They published my first articles on Silicon Valley and technology. Steve Kovachs was a brilliant editor. It was his edits that helped turn "That's It, I'm Finished Defending Sexism in Tech" from a niche blog post into an essay that was meaningful to a broader readership.

I owe that piece, and much of my writing in the last year, to Alex Wilhelm. It was his enthusiasm for the craft of writing that often propelled me to sit down at my laptop and type. He (informally) edited many of my pieces in late 2013 and early 2014, often making my writing and my arguments much more cogent and logically consistent. He also gave me lots of advice that might sound dumb reprinted here, out of context, but I can attest that it was absolutely the thing I needed to hear at the time.

I am also deeply appreciative of the investors, advisors and collaborators who have believed in me, and made my entrepreneurship (and so many shared projects, shared visions, companies) possible. I may be "leaning out," but I'm not doing it alone.

Elissa Shevinsky, aka #LADYBOSS, is a serial entrepreneur known for her work building cyber-security applications as well as her unique perspective on women in tech.